SAVAGE PILGRIMS

Henry Shukman

SAVAGE PILGRIMS

on the road to santa fe

KODANSHA INTERNATIONAL
New York • Tokyo • London

Kodansha America, Inc.
114 Fifth Avenue, New York, New York 10011, U.S.A.

Kodansha International Ltd.
17-14 Otowa 1-chome, Bunkyo-ku, Tokyo 112, Japan

Published in 1997 by Kodansha America, Inc.

Originally published in 1996 by HarperCollins*Publishers* Ltd., London.

Library of Congress Cataloging-in-Publication Data

Shukman, Henry.
    Savage pilgrims: on the road to Santa Fe / Henry Shukman.
        p.   cm.
    ISBN 1-56836-170-X (hc: alk. paper)
    1. Southwest, New—Description and travel—Anecdotes. 2. Shukman,
Henry—Journeys—Southwest, New—Anecdotes. I. Title.
F787.S52   1997
917.904'33—dc21   96-47446

Manufactured in the United States of America on acid-free paper

97 98 99 00 BERT/B 10 9 8 7 6 5 4 3 2 1

Contents

801294

A NOTE ON THE TITLE

When D. H. Lawrence reached New Mexico in 1922, he decided that his 'savage pilgrimage', his rambling worldwide search for a powerful pre-civilized culture, was finally over. New Mexico, he declared, was the only place that ever changed him from the outside. Since then, and indeed before then, innumerable people, one of them the author of this book, have made or have dreamt of making the same journey to the south-west.

SAVAGE PILGRIMS

PROLOGUE

Desert Dreams

I MET FRANKIE when I was twenty-two, and I could hardly believe my luck. She was a wild artist from New York City, a peroxide blonde who wore black miniskirts and silver space-age ankle-boots fit only for the Manhattan sidewalks. She sang for an underground rock band, was three years older than me, and taught me all kinds of things I had never imagined before. We met in London, exchanged one long kiss, and the day after she flew home she called me from across the ocean.

Our first telephone conversation, she in Manhattan, and I in my mother's house, in a quiet English village: 'I want to see you. Come over here.' Her words came down the satellite line as a whisper.

'What?'

There was a pause. 'I can't wait to see you.' Another pause. 'Come over here.'

She was actually asking me to go to New York to see her. I couldn't believe it. Nor could I go, but a month later she came to England with her family to celebrate Labor Day. I caught the train up to London dressed in my brother's dinner jacket on a cold, rosy evening, the sky darkening slowly, the west showing pale through the bushes lining the tracks. The little train panted across Buckinghamshire towards Marylebone station, and by the time the brick walls of London were rolling past it was getting dark.

At eight o'clock I made my way to the Dorchester Hotel, where Frankie's wealthy stepfather had booked a sixteen-place table for all of his extended family. At midnight Frankie sat down on the edge of the queen-size bed in her room and unbuttoned her shirt. At twelve-thirty someone knocked at the door. Just then her ankles were positioned right under my chin, shackled by her leggings, and she was wailing softly into my ear. All of which, the position no less than its effect, was new to me.

We stopped and listened. The knock came again.

'Who is it?'

'It's me.' It was her elder sister. Apparently she didn't know what to say next. 'I wondered what happened to you.' She hesitated. 'You're doing it, aren't you? Oh well. I guess I'm going to bed.'

You're doing it. A sister just saying it. *Oh well*. I didn't know people could talk like that. These people were truly uninhibited, quite unlike anyone I had ever known before. And it suddenly struck me that right then and there I was forging a link with them, driving an iron stake into their rock to tether myself to.

Two days after that Frankie called to tell me: 'We better just grab the bull by the horns. No sense waiting around.'

We flew to America the next day.

Coffee, whisky, sex, ketchup – even the same things tasted different in America. Sunsets looked different. They were brilliant and cold and spoke of big spaces and made you feel hollow, like a wind was blowing through you. I remembered one in particular. Frankie was in New York City and I was three hours away on Long Island, staying with a friend in a wooden cottage among the dunes. She had just called to say she was missing me. I hadn't seen her in a week. Soon I was planning to go north to work on a fishing boat, and I had been staying out in the country while she completed a big canvas in the city.

'I miss you,' her soft voice breathed down the line. 'I miss all of you.'

I knew what she was talking about. I could already feel the gentle weight of her breasts on my chest.

I went out for a walk, my legs shaking as I shuffled down the sand dunes. Inside the house they were heating sake on the wood stove, cooking broccoli and garlic chicken. Outside it was cold and dark was falling. The trees across the inlet were already black, and the sand was a pale glow, insubstantial. The black water carried the most fragile image of light, like gold leaf spread across the surface, or like a saucer of mercury trembling as someone carries it across a room. But up above, the sky was a defiant display of orange and crimson and lime. The colours had been applied in big strokes ignoring the laws of the spectrum, lying where they wished. Across them scrawled the fantastic graffiti of jets entering and leaving Kennedy Airport. Once a jet winked at me, a brilliant star at the front of a twin line, and vanished. Then I saw, through the black trees across the water, a blurry, pallid shape, a fleece hung in the trees. It startled me, even though I knew it was the moon.

I was jubilant. I went north to Portland, Maine, and found work on a trawler called the *Nordsee*. We were lucky and kept running into schools of monkfish, which were fetching high prices that season. After a month I had two thousand dollars, more money than I had ever had before. Frankie came up to join me and we moved inland. I got a job at a local airport in Vermont, and Frankie took a studio in a converted warehouse.

Every morning at seven thirty I went out into the cold fall air, jumped into the airport Jeep and rattled down the hills to work. I didn't come back till night, when Frankie and I would watch videos and drink vodka and Michelob and make love, while outside our cabin the leaves turned yellow then gold then red, as the autumn fell on Vermont.

Sometimes I went to visit her in her studio. The big high hall had been partitioned into a number of work spaces. Pictures had been pinned up on the screens dividing them, and you could hear a continual soft babble of relaxed chatter and laughter as the artists worked away. Frankie used to work on the floor of her unit, with a wheeled lamp and pots of her various odd materials spread out around her, among rags, sponges, rulers and old pens. Instead of using paints, she was experimenting at the time with beeswax, old tea, tar and glue, and recently she had found a bag of school erasers by the roadside, which she had taken to carving up and using as printing stamps in her pictures.

One Saturday afternoon I found her laying out black and white monoprints on top of one another, ready for storing. A fat roll of duct tape sat beside her. Her ponytail was unusually bright just then, radiant gold in the chalky air of the hall. I bent down, lifted it, and kissed her neck. She let out a soft laugh, but didn't look at me. She was warm like she was in bed after sex. Her fingers were smudged with ink and she was arranging the sheets carefully by the edge, using only her fingertips. She set another picture down and I picked up her left hand. The grey-silver ink smears highlighted the grain of her fingers, made them look metal. I kissed the tips and let the hand go. She stayed as she was, not unhappy that I was there, but not wanting to break her attention either.

From a corner of the room came a high peal of laughter. Then a man walked in. He had fair hair cut very short, and blond stubble on his jaw, picked out by the curiously illuminating light in the hall. His face was somewhat rounded, but tanned and suave-looking. He was a little plump, but he carried it smoothly, and it suited him. There was a self-possession about him, an ease, that was immediately appealing.

He glanced at me, smiling faintly. It looked like the kind of smile he would always have on his face. Then he looked down at Frankie. 'I've got it,' he said. He was holding a small clay sculpture by his side. The subject of the piece was hidden in his hand.

'Hi, Joel.' She didn't look up, but stayed hunched over, squatting, fingering her paintings. 'Joel, this is Henry.'

Joel stepped towards me and held out his hand. Something made me hesitate before taking it.

'How's it going?' he asked her.

'Fine.'

4

The three of us were silent a moment, listening to the rustle of her stiff papers.

'You can put it down over there,' she said.

She meant the little wooden cabinet by the door. He set the sculpture down. The clay made a quiet thud. It was a female nude reclining with one leg straight, the knee of the other raised, all done with rough knife-marks. It was a good piece. The proportions were right and it had a certain relaxed sophistication. I knew right away that it was Frankie. It surprised me. She hadn't told me she was modelling for anyone.

Joel glanced at her, then smiled at me steadily.

'So, Henry,' he said, apparently at ease, 'What do you do?'

'Right now I'm between boats,' I said. I liked the expression. It hinted at a painful separation, though I had no intention of returning to fishing boats, and it sounded better than cleaning the toilets and pumping gas at an airport.

Joel glanced at my shoes – roughed-up deck shoes from K-Mart – and nodded. I asked what he did. He shrugged his shoulders. His blue-grey eyes rested easily on mine. 'I'm an artist. I paint pictures and make things. Things I like.'

A streak of sunlight found my left cheek from a high window. I stepped out of it. 'Do you make a living like that?'

'You don't need money where I live.'

'Where do you live?' My voice sounded higher than I wanted.

'New Mexico.'

'How can you live without money?'

'Come to New Mexico and see. It's a cool place.' He chuckled. 'The coolest. The only place for an artist. Where else is there? Forget New York and LA. Forget Europe. Europe's all over. Santa Fe's the only real community right now. It's Paris in the '20s all over again. You know where I live? At the foot of the Blood of Christ Mountains. That's what they call them. The Sangre de Cristos. Every dawn and sunset they turn red as, red as –' He shrugged. 'As red as blood.'

He arranged to meet up with Frankie later. I watched him as he walked towards the door, moving slowly and easily and somehow brightly, as if bathed perpetually in his own private sunbeam. I couldn't help feeling curiously privileged to have met him. This artist from New Mexico had breezed over to Vermont, made some sculptures, some things he liked, and soon would ride back to the south-west, to the land of the free.

It got me thinking about New Mexico. Frankie sometimes talked about the Four Corners region of the south-west, where she had gone hiking when she was eighteen. She showed me a photograph she had taken there of an adobe farmhouse. Its wicket fence and window frames and front door were all painted with the same peeling blue-green paint, a good colour against the adobe walls. I liked the photograph, and began to imagine living in such a house with Frankie. She would paint there and I would support us with some kind of simple labour, in a bar or on a farm. Not only that, but Frankie's eyes were the same colour as that green paint. They even had the same chipped and peeled look when you studied them closely.

I started dreaming about New Mexico. I had one particularly vivid dream in which I was a poet who lived in a large studio with white floorboards. I was sitting on a cushion on the floor with a girlfriend facing me, a blue china teapot steaming between us. Outside there was silent desert all around, and a high still sky, and I felt profound contentment, living a life that suited me. My girlfriend could feel the calm in me too, and loved me for it.

I woke up from the dream and lay beside Frankie in the pre-dawn dark on our mattress, sure that New Mexico was the place for us. The Atlantic was a harsh ocean, and created lives to match for its people. Britain, New England, Scandinavia were countries where you needed Viking and Teuton genes, so the rain in your eyes made you feel tough, not cold. I had lived in the north too long, I suddenly realized. Further west, nearer the Pacific, in the desert of the south-west, I would be able to lead a warm, quiet life, something very different, something I wanted.

Once a month a priest used to fly into the airport. He was known as the Flying Father and flew a Mooney, a fast, single-engine plane with a cut-back tail and retractable landing gear, the most desirable of all small planes, making his way across America on some obscure mission, stopping off here and there to lead certain congregations in their worship – in Iowa, Indiana, the Dakotas, Illinois, as well as Vermont. His home town was Carrizozo, New Mexico.

I liked him. He would come taxiing briskly to the pumps and tell me to fill her up. 'Always like to be ready for a quick getaway,' he would explain with a chuckle. He had a lined suntanned face, cropped silver hair and steely eyes, and looked as though he had been toughened and cured by the New Mexican skies. He always wore a black poloneck and exuded a bright, tough spirituality, as if he came out of a pure, ascetic life in the south-western desert. I asked him what it was like out there, and he told me, 'You better come and see for yourself some day.'

Meanwhile Frankie was becoming withdrawn. We talked less and less. Often she didn't get back from her studio till late, and sometimes she spent the night there. Then one Saturday a gale blew all night long. We woke up on Sunday morning to find our cabin no longer standing in a forest, but in a desert of stark tree trunks. It was as if the house were suddenly floodlit. The living room, which previously had seemed heavy and dark with its drapes, was suddenly bright, and grime marks had appeared on the door of the fridge overnight, while the kitchen sink looked whiter than ever before. What had been a lawn outside was a marsh of leaves.

We sat at the table with cups of coffee steaming brightly between our fingers. One of us was going to make pancakes, neither yet felt ready to do it. Things had been getting increasingly strained between us, and in the unforgiving clarity of that first morning of winter we both knew the time had come to do something about it.

But we had different ideas about what to do. Frankie got up from the table and climbed into the sleeping loft. I heard a tap running in the bathroom, then her clicking tread moving to the bed. From the knocks and creakings of the floor, and the rustlings, I could tell that she was going back and forth between the closet and the bed.

She came down the ladder with a suitcase, said she would call me in a couple of days, and left. I heard her truck start up and sit there idling for a while, as if she wasn't sure whether to move off, then the sound of the engine drew away. I sat watching the white steam from my coffee cup rise through the air of what had been our dark kitchen, and tried to lift the cup to my lips, but couldn't summon the will.

Then on a sudden impulse I ran outside, leapt into the Jeep and skidded off down the track. I guessed that she was probably heading back to New York, and once I hit the tarmac at the bottom of the hill I slammed my foot down and roared towards town, which she would have to pass through on her way south. She didn't have more than a couple of minutes' start on me. I overtook a Buick station wagon, then a purple Volkswagen Jetta, then settled into the long smooth stretch of easy bends that eventually delivered you to the white steeple of the Episcopalian church on the edge of town. I had just passed the church when I saw her truck up ahead.

She had parked at the roadside. I drew up alongside and looked in. It was empty. I drove on a little further and thought about what to do. She might have stopped to buy something, in which case I could find her when she came out of whichever shop it was. Or she might have decided to move into town, in one of the clapboard houses on the street, most likely the one she had parked outside, in which case perhaps I should go and knock on the door. But who would answer? What would I say to them? And I hadn't even begun to think about what I would actually say to Frankie. All I knew was that I didn't want it to end like this.

My deliberations were cut short when Frankie came out of the house followed by a man, the sculptor, Joel. He carried two kitbags slung over either shoulder, and held a wide shallow box in front. I saw her attempt to take the box. He shook his head. She went ahead and opened the back of the truck, where he deposited his belongings, while she climbed into the cab and leant across to unlock his door.

It was an overcast day, very cold. Winter had truly arrived now in New England. My breath came out in a cloud of steam and fogged up the windows, which I wiped clear with my elbow. Joel was wearing a dark-grey car coat and a pair of green slacks. I watched him rub his hands together and blow on them, then pull open his door. I wondered where they were going, then suddenly understood. A day like this, the first day of winter in Vermont – it was the perfect day to begin a long road trip. It was a day on which to leave for the desert. Joel, with his bronze face and short blond hair, didn't belong in a northern winter. He was migrating now, going back home to the sunny desert, and Frankie was going with him.

I was shocked. I sat still, not knowing what to do. The truck's headlights came on, and they drove right past me without noticing. The traffic light was green and they drove straight on through. A neat little tail of exhaust smoke fluttered in the cold air behind them, like a train of tin cans tied to a wedding car.

I didn't move. I felt like I had lost a layer of clothing, or a layer of skin. A long warm night was over and now I was waking to the cold light of day. I felt like I was standing under a new sky. Nothing seemed familiar.

I got out and wandered around town, acutely aware of all sights and sounds and sensations. Two icy grips had seized my wrists where the cuffs of my jacket ended. An aeroplane droned noisily by overhead, hidden in low clouds, sounding fat and slow like a bumblebee, and I realized I knew it was a Cessna 152. I had subconsciously learnt the different plane noises at the airport. The cars, the houses, the trees, all seemed to have had a film shaved off them by the cold. Then I heard a bell clanging nearby, and dumbly turned down a side street towards the sound.

It was coming from a modern church called the Reformed Catholic Assembly. The doors were wide open and I walked straight into the brightly lit interior, where a woman with short black hair and a string of pearls smiled at me and pointed me to a pew at the back. I slumped down.

By chance it turned out to be the Flying Father's church. He came walking up the aisle, wearing a black jacket over his usual poloneck, and a silver cross on a chain, shaking hands and murmuring greetings, then took his stand at the front. 'Where there are no oxen,' his deep voice boomed, 'the crib is clean.' He went on to explain the proverb, but I found it hard to listen. It had something to do with not being able to make an omelette without breaking eggs. I didn't take much of the service in, but it seemed full of the resigned Old Testament wisdom of Amos and Ecclesiastes. The cross and the mass were mere afterthoughts, while the real message was of the acceptance of suffering. 'Vanity, vanity, all is vanity': he was a preacher in that tradition.

Afterwards he stood in the doorway, offering solace to the departing congregation, blessing them both with his words and with the fine matutinal incense of his bacon-scented breath, which rose up in clouds into the cold. When my turn came he recognized me and gave me an encouraging smile.

'All well?' he asked.

'Not really,' I answered. I told him my girlfriend had just left me.

He listened, paused and said softly, 'Put hand to the plough. You're an educated fellow. Enough summer-jobbing.' He chuckled quietly. 'I'm sure they're waiting for you back home.'

I walked back to the Jeep feeling numb and dazed. But I was also aware of a little question mark resting like an uncertain smile on my breast.

I saw him the next morning at the airport, as he was leaving. He performed a cursory pre-flight check, stooping under the wings of his Mooney, then clambered into the cockpit and sent me a wave before he slid the glass shut. Then he did a clearance takeoff, whether out of pure exuberance or because he guessed I was still watching I never knew. Either way, it brought a smile to my lips to see him get the nose up, level off at ten feet and scream along the runway with the undercarriage tucked up like a fighter plane, then suddenly yank the Mooney into a banking climb. He did a barrel roll and disappeared into the next valley on his quest.

New Mexico. The next day or the day after he might be there. I thought of him alone in his cockpit, his cropped suntanned head, his grip stowed on the back seat, just him and his wings high above the desert. It made my heart beat faster. He had a life to aspire to.

Eventually, over the following days, I realized that I had two choices. Either I went out to New Mexico and tried to find Frankie, in the hope of winning her back, or I went home. Then gradually it became clear that the Flying Father was right and I really only had one choice. A month later I left America.

Six years passed, during which I moved through a variety of jobs in England. But I never gave up on my hope of one day going to New Mexico, perhaps even of living there, and although I sometimes took time off to go travelling, in the hope that it might calm my dim craving, it didn't work.

I hadn't ever heard from Frankie again, but what finally decided me was coming upon the remains of an old T-shirt she had given me. It was on a Sunday night in London, after I had spent a rainy weekend elsewhere, while I was unpacking my bag. All that was left of the shirt was a square of cotton the size of a handkerchief, printed with a design of a Navajo rug, which I had cut from the front. I thought I had lost it years ago, but it had rolled itself into a tight scroll and lain in hiding in a seldom-used compartment of the bag. I opened it out on the bed.

It came from Taos, New Mexico, and had long been my favourite shirt, till it split along the seams and in order to save the design I cut the rest of it away. The rug was a weaving of amber and brown stripes with a row of tassels at the bottom, just below which the words 'Navajo Serape by Bigfoot Walker' had been handwritten in slanting capitals.

I had had other mementoes of my time in America with Frankie – an eagle feather from the Delaware woods, a finger-pull from a Manhattan manhole, a misshapen grey pearl that I extracted from an oyster caught in a trawling net off Maine – but I lost all of them. As the years went by I thought I had lost this one too. The sight of it, and the feel of the fine cotton, seemed to knock me to my senses like a cold shower. My pulse quickened. I thought of the Flying Father, of Joel, of Frankie, and wondered what had happened to them all. There was a world across the ocean that I had once been on the verge of entering. Just then I could not understand why I hadn't entered it back then, six years ago, when I had wanted to. I still wanted to.

I rolled the cloth up and went to the window. A flyover below stretched away to the south-west, and somewhere down that way, beyond the orange-grey smudge of London sky, the desert of America was just now basking in a strong morning sun, and a man with cropped silver hair was surely sliding shut the cover of a cockpit over his head, preparing to launch himself into the sky.

ONE

A High Township

DOLLY AND CHARLENE, her daughter, met me at the airport in Alamogordo. I saw them standing beside a large cruising truck in the carpark by the small, grey terminal building, clutching hats to their heads while a fierce wind whipped their dresses about.

They were friends of a friend, and were living in a farmhouse in Cloudcroft for the summer. Cloudcroft, Dolly told me on the wide two-lane road that wound up off the desert, was the highest township in the United States. Or the western states, she wasn't sure. Certainly the highest in New Mexico, anyway.

We went into a long uphill tunnel. When we emerged at the other end we had passed out of one landscape and into another. Gone were the rust-coloured ravines, the Algarve cacti and the strewn boulders of the desert, supine beneath its gypsum sky. Now the world was green. There were fir trees and little meadows, and in the distance high, bare, green slopes catching a gleam of sunshine, the kind of slopes you might expect to see an ibex or chamois traverse. The sky had changed, too. It was full of white clouds passing over a deep blue, and you sensed that rain had fallen recently. It was a boisterous, fecund sky now, alpine.

In Cloudcroft itself everything was housed in wooden chalets: the cashier of the Texaco station sat in a little pine chalet, across the road the row of shops with Cliff's Bakery and Somerwell Realty were roofed with pitched, stained beams and overhanging eaves.

As the sun lowered behind the treetops I wound up my window. It was cold out, even now in late July. The two local industries were cattle, which were driven off the mountains in September, and skiing.

We drove through town and on for five miles, meandering along a valley with a narrow strip of meadows flanked by fir. Every four hundred yards we passed a gate. Off down a track you would see a red farmhouse with a porch. Now and then a cabin swung into view, low, heavily wooden, the kind of dwelling from which pesky old men in braces emerge in cowboy films, brandishing a bottle of whiskey. My spirits lifted when I saw them. They reminded me of *Alias Smith and Jones*, which I had watched religiously every Monday night as a child, a comedy series about the escapades of two lovable outlaws, Hannibal Hayes and Kid Curry. Here I was in their country. One of the actors, Pete Duel, later committed suicide, which had only increased my devotion to the reruns.

Soon we were bumping down a farm track.

'We're in the bunkhouse,' Dolly said, and laughed. It was a joke.

'Dormitory-style,' I said, to confirm it.

They both laughed. We were making for a modest-looking modern home with a large porch. In the yard in front stood a silver caravan. After a pause Dolly said, 'Actually, you've got a choice. There's a pullout in the living room, or some foam you could put down, and there's even a trailer if you want some peace and quiet.'

We did not get off to a good start. The friend who had given me Dolly's name was a young Greek art dealer from New York called Gust. Dolly was one of his clients. She was an abstract artist in middle age, a good painter, and friendly and hospitable. But Gust had not told me the whole story.

No sooner had Dolly installed me on an imitation leather couch on the porch than she asked, 'So how did you meet Gust?'

Innocently I answered, 'Through Tasmin.'

'Tasmin?'

'His girlfriend.'

This did not elicit the polite smile I expected. Dolly choked on her Amstel Light. She wiped her thin mouth with the back of her hand and said, 'His what?'

I coughed. 'His girlfriend.'

'Tasmin is his girlfriend,' she stated, though it was a question.

'You haven't met her?'

'I didn't know he had a *girl*friend,' she said, with an odd emphasis on the word. Then she looked away across the meadow, which stretched to the fir slopes on the far side. I followed her gaze. The white clouds in the sky had coagulated, and now the evening was overcast, but the sun had found a gap somewhere low on the horizon and silver light flooded the valley. The meadow looked like it was covered with dew, and the two horses standing in the field glistened. The nearer of them, a bay mare, cropped close, shivered, and I saw the sheen flex over its muscles. It was a beautiful valley, and it was high in the mountains of New Mexico. For a moment I had that dizzying sense of freedom that high mountains can give, when the thin, cool air makes you feel light and agile and capable at last of doing all the things that really matter. Your life down in the lowlands seems like child's play, easily manageable. But it was only a moment.

'He has a girlfriend,' Dolly repeated.

'Sure he does.' I wondered if perhaps she thought Gust was gay. I could clarify the matter for her. 'She's very nice,' I added.

Dolly turned and sent me a smile that pinned me to the couch. She rose abruptly from her rocking chair in the corner of the porch and without a word walked into the house.

Ten minutes passed. I didn't know what to do. I hoped that perhaps she had suddenly remembered a pot on the stove or a telephone call that couldn't wait. With every minute that went by it became less and less likely. Should I wait? Should I go in and apologize for something? For what? Or was she sick?

I waited another five minutes then went in.

I found her seated cross-legged on a cushion in front of a blazing fire. She had her hands resting palm upwards on either knee and was completely still. There was a strange stillness in the room, too. As I walked in and saw her I became acutely aware right away of the sound of the flames, and of the clock ticking above the fridge. It was as if I had walked into a temple, and in the awed hush every sound became clear and imminent.

Darkness was falling now. It was seven o'clock. I had been hoping to make a cup of tea and suggest either going out to supper or making something here. But the kitchen was part of the living room, and it seemed impossibly disrespectful to run a tap now and switch on the gas and fill a pan, with her meditating before the fire. Nor could I very well talk to her. I stepped back out on to the porch.

Two kittens scampered over to me, and strutted between my legs. I sat on the couch and they jumped into my lap purring so vigorously their bodies shook. I waited with my fingers on their trembling shoulders.

Dolly can't have been younger than forty-five, but it was a youthful forty-five. She was slim, even slight, and had a taut, sun-creased face. There wasn't an ounce of excess flesh on her frame, and her tight jaw-line described the perfect dog-leg to her chin. She had narrow powder-blue eyes. In her tight jeans and denim jacket she made a fine cowgirl.

She was born here in south-eastern New Mexico but had lived in New York for twenty years, and it had inevitably rubbed off. She wore a kimono around the house, drank herb teas instead of cowboy coffee, and practised Zen meditation. She had come out to New Mexico just for the summer, subletting her loft in SoHo and renting the house till October. As a child she had lived first in west Texas, which was only two hours away, then in Alamogordo. She used to come up to Cloudcroft for summer holidays and to ski. They had moved to Alamogordo because her daddy was in the Air Force, and Alamogordo was home to USAF Holloman.

'Top Gun training ground,' she told me a little while later, when she joined me and the kittens on the porch.

Her daddy, who had started life as a cowboy, had become a test parachutist for the military, she added.

'A what?' I asked.

'Well, first he was a test pilot,' she explained in her soft, husky voice, in which you could just detect a trace of her childhood drawl. 'But then he wanted to do something a little, er –' she let out a gentle laugh. 'Er –' She gestured for the word.

'Braver?' I volunteered.

She smiled. 'Exactly. He's a man who enjoys a challenge. He was a champion bull-rider too, inciden'ally, as a boy. So anyways. He took to testing the latest prototype parachutes.'

I had never known that such a thing existed as a test parachutist. I had never thought about it before, but now it was obvious that someone had to do it.

'A test parachutist,' I repeated, letting the full impact sink in. I shook my head. 'You can't really get braver than that.'

She laughed lightly again. 'That's what he thought.'

After my difficult start with Dolly I seemed to be recovering. But it didn't last. There was an easel up in the living room, which held a canvas with an abstract design of dark green with three squares, one blue and two blank, where colour had yet to be applied. I was determined to make good the ground I seemed to be making, and when she asked me what I thought, I blurted out: 'It's marvellous, extremely promising, it's obviously going in exactly the right direction. It'll be great when it's finished.'

She was silent a moment. She laughed. 'I'm sorry?'

'I think it's excellent,' I said. I was about to go on, to explain myself, when I stopped. 'Excellent,' I muttered, letting the matter rest, and took a swig from the Amstel she had given me.

She eyed me for a moment, a wry smile stretching her lips, when I was saved by Charlene, her daughter, walking into the room. She had been sleeping since we arrived.

17

Charlene looked at me. 'You feeling OK? The altitude didn't do you in?'

'Fine, thanks, Charlene.'

She was a flaming redhead with bright emerald eyes, in her early twenties – Dolly must have had her young – and she quickly informed me that although her mother was allowed to call her Charlene, she preferred the name Charlie. She had grown up in New York and now went to college there. She didn't need a cowgirl name any more, she said, something out of a Country and Western song.

'I'm always telling her it's a perfectly good name,' Dolly said. 'But I don't know. If she wants to change it. . .'

'Mom.' Charlie glared at her.

She was an angry young woman. It was easy for Dolly to get her going, almost any issue would do, and she would turn into a livid sibyl with fierce eyes possessed by every known form of disgruntlement.

'So she got you a beer anyway,' Charlie said. She went down to the fridge to get herself one too. The three of us sat down on the chairs in the living room with the night fallen now outside. It was an odd moment, sitting with two strangers in their summer house at night up in the mountains near the Texas border. There was an awkward silence. I still felt distinctly uneasy with Dolly. I wanted to make her like me better, but didn't know how. Conversation didn't pick up much, and Dolly soon got up saying she would make us a stir-fry.

'Oh, goody,' Charlie said. 'Mom makes an excellent stir-fry.'

I helped with cleaning and chopping the vegetables.

After supper I decided to sleep in the trailer parked outside. Although Charlie chattered away obliviously, there was still an acute awkwardness between myself and Dolly. Throughout dinner she had sat quite still with that faint smile moulded into her thin lips, and hardly said a word. Was this simply the way she was, I wondered, or was it me? And what should I do to put things right? At least I could be out of her way at night, I thought, sleeping under a separate roof.

She gave me sheets and a towel and as I strolled across the yard I felt, to my surprise, the very same wry smile that had been on Dolly's face settling on my own lips. I couldn't understand it. Did I think that Dolly's coolness was some odd kind of welcoming test for me, or that it was faintly humorous to have insulted her eye as a painter? Or was it the whole situation that seemed comic – to be going out to sleep in a chrome trailer in the yard of a mother and daughter I had never met before in the highlands of New Mexico? And why was that funny?

The trailer swayed a little as I entered, and each step I took made it sink slightly on its springs. Her father had brought it up from El Paso a month ago so he and his wife could stay the odd weekend. He had retired to the west Texas town now, where he spent his time writing essays on the history of the West for academic journals. One of them, the *History Review of New Mexico, Southeast*, lay beside the plastic sink. I reached for it from my bed. There he was: P. D. Morton. And the essay: 'Did Henry McCarty Pass Through Cloudcroft in 1877?'

The said Henry McCarty, also known as Henry Antrim, had apparently been caught thieving in Silver City, some eighty miles away. His first theft had been several pounds of butter, the next a bundle of clothes from a Chinese laundry, after which he had been put in jail, though not for long. The editor of the local newspaper said of the arrest, and subsequent ingenious escape: 'Henry McCarty, who was arrested upon the charge of stealing clothes from Charley Sun and Sam Chung, celestials, sans cue, sans Joss sticks, escaped from prison yesterday through the chimney. It's believed that Henry was simply the tool of "Sombrero Jack", who done the stealing whilst Henry done the hiding. Jack has skinned out.' Henry was to skin out too, first westwards into Arizona, and then back east, into the mountains of Lincoln County, New Mexico, just a small way east of where I now was. The question posed in the essay was whether or not he would have made his way there by passing through Cloudcroft, but the argument was mostly speculation. Whichever way he went, by the time he reached Lincoln, he had changed his name to the more familiar William H. Bonney, or Billy the Kid.

I read two pages then switched out the light and lay in the dark feeling the strange lucid wakefulness of high altitude, and listened to a screech owl somewhere out in the woods. It reminded me of the forests of Poland, to which my family had made a pilgrimage when I was eleven, visiting the land from which my father's folks had come. We had stayed in a village of wooden houses built at the foot of a long slope of fir. It was the kind of forest I had read about in Russian folk tales, where you might come across the witch Baba Yaga's hut, perched on its single chicken leg.

When I rolled over in bed the trailer leaned slightly, like a boat. For an instant I thought it might topple, but it only sighed a little.

TWO

Rodeo Knights

CHARLIE MADE BLUEBERRY pancakes and strong coffee in the morning. After breakfast she settled on the porch with her book, the memoirs of the eleventh-century Japanese courtesan Sei Shonagan, and Dolly opened up the French windows, got out her brushes and examined her painting. I withdrew to the trailer.

Over lunch I asked Dolly about Santa Fe and Taos in northern New Mexico.

She shrugged her shoulders. 'It's all hot tubs and kitsch art.'

'Is that where the earth is red?'

'Sure. And the BMWs and the Range Rovers are brand new. And it's full of galleries, and the galleries are full of schlock.' She stabbed her fork into her Caesar salad. 'I can't stand it. I used to go up there, but this is so much more – more *real*. This is the real New Mexico. Cowboys and working people and cold nights. Up there it's the chocolate-box New Mexico. You'll see.'

'But isn't it beautiful?'

'Piñon and desert and stuff. It's OK, but it's a *scene*,' she said. 'There's no scene here.'

Charlie chimed in, 'It's fake. It's so fake you can't believe it. It's like tourist bullshit, the whole thing, Indians, cowboys, cactus, coyotes – if you can sell it, use it. And the suckers keep on coming, keep on lapping it up. Texans,' she added, disgusted.

'Charlene. Don't forget where we come from.'

'We come from Alamogordo, New Mexico, Mom. What are you talking about?'

'Your granddaddy lives in El Paso and, as you know, he was born in Midland, Texas.'

Charlie didn't reply. She drained her glass of iced tea.

'Midland?' I said. 'I had a friend who lived there for a while.' Ten years ago a friend of my brother's had gone to Midland to try to break into the oil business. It had been an oil boom town then, with the most successful Rolls-Royce dealership in the world. 'How is it these days?'

'Ain't what it used to be. But if you need cheap office space, get yourself over there. Yessir.'

It was after lunch that I finally had my first glimpse of Dolly's true colours, of how she really liked to be treated by men. In my nervousness I had studiously avoided looking either Dolly or Charlene in the eye for too long, in case they interpreted it as a chauvinistic come-on. My judgment couldn't have been more wrong.

While we were clearing the table on the porch, Ralph, the retired rancher who rented them the house, strolled across the field towards us. He came up to the porch with a Swishers Sweet Wood-Tip cigar in hand, the packet in breast pocket, and doffed his stetson. All the local men wore cowboy hats, either of white straw or black felt. Ralph had the black kind. He wore a button-down shirt, a pair of dirty jeans on a pair of skinny legs, and beaten-up old boots. I half expected him to say, 'Well how dee, li'l lady.'

Instead he announced, 'My God, did we take a batterin' yesterday.' He was referring to the rainstorm of the previous afternoon, of which I had seen the aftermath. 'Six inches.' He shook his head. 'And how is ever'thin' over here?'

'We're doing fine, Ralph,' said Dolly. Her voice had changed. She was speaking much more firmly, more demonstratively than usual. Her drawl had acquired a distinct twang.

'Kittens been botherin' you?' He meant the farmyard kittens that I had seen the day before. Sometimes they skipped across the meadow to Dolly's porch.

'They've been over here. There's one we call Cowboy because he says thank you when we feed him.'

Ralph didn't so much as blink at the compliment. 'Well, you need 'nything you let us know.' His face creased in a smile.

As he walked off Dolly told me, 'Ralph's part Navajo. You can just see it.'

I couldn't, but she said it took practice. There was a certain smoothness about his face. Although it was tough and leathery it was not wrinkled, she said, and his complexion, what you could see of it through the wind and sun tan, was pale and fine.

As Ralph's figure grew smaller across the meadow, Dolly followed it with her eyes. 'Me and my big ideas,' she murmured. 'SoHo galleries and the Whitney Museum. I should have stayed right here and got myself a cowboy.'

Just then, in the field, Ralph slapped the bay mare on the rump. She twitched and he reached down to pat her cheek as she grazed. Dolly sighed.

As it happened it was a Saturday, and a good idea struck me. I asked them both out for a drink that night. We could go to the smart golfing and skiing hotel that we had driven past in Cloudcroft. Dolly had said it was a popular haunt for the Top Guns at the base.

They both eagerly accepted and told me to leave everything alone when I attempted to help with the washing up.

'You leave us to do it,' Dolly said, giving me a little smile that said something different from the wry one I had seen up till now. I walked over to the trailer feeling unexpectedly delighted.

It rained in the afternoon. The drops, distinct like little pellets, more distinct, more pronounced than rain ever is in England, drummed loudly on the roof of the trailer. It was like being in a tent. When we set off in Dolly's Dodge Ram Charger at six o'clock, the track up to the road was a chute of mud. After a moment's hesitation I offered to take the wheel. The suggestion was met at once with smiles of gratitude. Now the heavy, powerful truck was sliding from side to side. I slipped it into four-wheel drive and we whined up the rest of the way without getting stuck.

We started in the bar of the Lodge Hotel, a complete mountaintop resort with its own golf course and ski lifts. On the walls hung signed photographs of astronauts in space suits holding their helmets against their chests, and autographed pictures of silver starfighters banking over cloud ranges. Beneath their names the pilots had written down their identification numbers and the nicknames of their planes: 'Pretty Polly,' one said. 'Dynamic Duo,' claimed a picture of a twin-engine reconnaissance plane. And a third declared, enigmatically: 'Placebo Gazebo.'

Dolly and Charlene at once seated themselves on stools and leaned over the wooden bar on their elbows in anticipation of their drinks. As I looked at Dolly in her denim skirt, her slim torso resting against the bar, the heels of her suede cowboy boots caught on the rung of the stool, I suddenly found myself imagining her walking out to the trailer with me at night. I put the thought out of my mind. It was ridiculous. Yet somehow it wasn't hard to imagine.

I ordered margaritas for them and a Rolling Rock for myself. I had unwittingly designated myself the driver for the night, I now realized, and their eager acceptance of my offer to take the wheel appeared in a new light. While placing the drinks on napkins in front of them, the barman smiled as if to say that he need hardly state what a pleasure it was to serve such charming ladies. He nudged my beer across to me, followed by a frosted mug. I watched the mist clear as I poured out the bottle. A sludge of frozen beer rose to the top of the glass. It looked inviting.

Although it was after six it was still light outside. It seemed early to be drinking, as if we were having cognac at tea time, but Dolly and Charlene drained off their cocktails before I had drunk down to the handle of my beer glass.

They ordered two more. Somewhere towards the end of the

second they got into a heated discussion about Charlie's father, Dolly's first husband, who had been a Texan no-hoper, from what I could gather, a would-be writer who now lived on Roosevelt Island in the middle of New York's East River.

I had missed the start of the argument and wasn't sure what points were being made, but Dolly seemed to be defending herself. 'All I was saying was, they are fine, honourable men. Always have been and always will be. You can't do better'n a cowboy.'

She paused at this point to smile to the barman, who above his white apron and black pants was wearing a snow-white stetson with a tuft of blue eagle down in the band. She took the opportunity to raise her eyebrows and shrug for another round, and threw down the remains of her second margarita.

Charlie was glaring at her. Her eyes had become fiercer than usual, as if outlined heavily with eyeliner, and so wide open you could see the white all the way round. She apparently had not taken well to the advice to find herself a cowboy. 'I'll do what the fuck I choose,' she said.

Dolly coughed. Charlie had not lowered her voice and the barman must have heard what she said. Scared of escalating the quarrel, Dolly didn't know what to say next. She picked up her glass again and tipped it back, even though it was empty. A silence rang at the bar. The only sounds were of tequila pouring over ice, then of ice rattling as the barman shook the drink, and finally of the bases of the fresh glasses clicking down on the bar-top.

'There you go, ladies,' he said.

They both thanked him, not quite in unison.

I offered a toast: 'Here's to free will, to doing whatever we want.'

I hoped it would be something they could both affirm, and they did indeed raise their glasses. Another silence followed. Then Dolly asked me what I was working on.

It was getting dark outside when we went downstairs to the basement bar, the Red Dog Saloon. A band was playing: three local girls had packed themselves into tight white trousers and satin cowboy shirts, sprayed their blonde hair into giant cumuli, and had taken the stage. They sang along to a tape of Beatles hits, set to a Country beat, in front of a handful of customers at the tables.

Ralph was sitting near the front with his wife. He swivelled round in his chair and touched his hat brim to Dolly. Now he was wearing a shirt, jeans, boots, hat, exactly as in the daytime, but they were all freshly laundered and pressed ones. We ordered more drinks, as well as burgers and fries. At the start of each song Ralph rose to ask his wife for the dance, then two-stepped back and forth in the strip right beneath the stage, spinning her round like a waltzer.

Dolly cooed over Ralph through her first two beers. He was the kind of man she ought to have found herself twenty years ago. Each time he rose from the table and offered his hand to his wife, Dolly looked away. There weren't more than ten other people in the place, all couples. After five or six songs it became clear there were no spare cowboys here tonight, and Dolly dropped a hint she knew a better place not far away called Desperado's, a dance hall down off the mountains in Alamogordo.

It took only half an hour of ear-popping descent for us to drop the thirty miles to Alamogordo. Desperado's parking lot was full of row upon row of pick-up trucks. There wasn't a car in the place. Under the glare of the lot's floodlights the trucks all looked the same colour, shape and size, as if we had driven into the compound of a truck factory.

The air was warm and carried the faintly bitter smell of the desert, a milky dustiness, a suggestion of chalk. A huge sign covered half the warehouse, illuminated by a row of lamps, but despite its size you could barely read the letters. They were lost in glare. As I walked closer, I discerned what it said: 'Desperado's. Dance With The Bulls.' The apostrophe was bigger than the letters.

The place had been built like a barn, on a tight budget, and decorated inside the same way. A bulk-buy of enamel fans hung from the ceiling, strings of fairy lights festooned the walls, which were covered with fake-wood wallpaper to give the appropriate western touch for the cowboys and cowgirls inside. There was hardly a person not wearing a stetson and boots, and between the legs of the crowd moved identically dressed children, miniature versions of their parents. The place was for everyone – singles, couples, even a family night out – provided they wore the regulation jeans, ropers and hat.

On the dance floor couples swiftly two-stepped to the music of a country band. The tables, cluttered with beer bottles and triangular margarita glasses, lay deserted, until the steel guitar wailed its last lament at the end of the song, whereupon everybody flowed off the dance floor back to their seats.

We stood with a pack of cowboys at the bar drinking Budweiser and watching the dancers, while Dolly and Charlene described two-stepping to me in detail. I tried to change the subject twice, having suddenly realized what was in store for me, but they unswervingly brought it round again. Two slow steps, two quick, Dolly said. You didn't move your body except below the belt, she added with a smile.

'Like salsa dancing,' Charlie threw in. You held the woman close. It was easy if someone showed you how.

I had no choice then. I figured I should ask Dolly first, she being the elder, and she didn't need to be asked twice. She tugged one of my hands into the small of her back, thrust the other up into the air, and launched us onto the floor. It was like bumper cars, everyone streaming round and round. The flow was counter-clockwise, but you could cut corners, slip across the middle, and you kept a keen eye out for other couples. Collisions occurred frequently, but no one seemed to mind. The really skilful would forestall them by spinning round, turning their momentum into rotation.

Dolly persevered. 'Two quick, two slow,' she would say in time to the beat I was supposed to be following, but she soon realized it was useless. I was a no-hoper. She smiled, but the disappointment was visible in her eyes. After only one song she let Charlie try me out, but she was equally shocked. Fortunately for them, I had at least served to demonstrate their readiness to dance to the press of cowboys at the bar, who were not slow to touch their hat-brims and offer their hands.

'You ready for some bootscootin', lady?' I heard one of them ask Dolly. She threw back her head and laughed, and the two of them spun off into the fray. 'The name's Rock,' another offered Charlie. She smiled back demurely, from under her brows, and gave him her hand.

Their various suitors began to console themselves, while the ladies were off dancing with other men, by sounding me out for information. 'They livin' here's then?' asked Ted from Montana, who used to play bass in a country band and who even in a pair of high cowboy heels barely made my chin. 'You sure they ain't sisters?' insisted Cliff from nearby Roswell, who ran a computer store and towered over the rest of the throng. 'So she is divorced, right?' checked Studs from Silver City, who wore dark glasses beneath his stetson and flew small commercial planes.

Gradually more and more beers appeared in front of me. 'A Silver Bullet for the gentleman,' I heard people call brightly to the barmaid, as if they were the first to have the idea. The beers were long-neck bottles of Coors Lite, not a strong brew, but still, I was unsure I could drink six of them before driving home.

Then a man bought me a shot of tequila. He raised himself from his stool a little way along from me, and came up with a salt-shaker and a slice of lime.

'The name's Horse,' he said. He was a big man, with straggly black hair and a thick moustache, and a friendly, if puffy, face. He held out a large hand. When I shook it I found it to be soft and warm. There was something reassuring in his grip. One sensed right away that he was a gentle giant.

'Been hearin' your accent,' he said. 'You a limey?'

I nodded and introduced myself.

28

Just then a friend of his approached us, a man in a suede hat with an odd blond moustache that had not been trimmed in a while, so the long bristles formed a sloping shelf over his lip. He had a bright pink face and small very blue eyes, in which a somewhat menacing sparkle played.

Horse said, 'This here's Dean. He works with me.'

'As a matter of fact, I work *for* him,' the man corrected. 'Hoss here's my boss. One of the biggest ranchers around. Ninety sections we run in all,' he said proudly, taking a swig from his Silver Bullet.

'What's a section?' I asked.

'Square mile. You a limey?'

'Yes.'

'Say "God Save the Queen."'

'What?'

'Just say it.'

I frowned, hesitating, then said it.

Dean slapped his thigh and let out a percussive laugh. 'By God, he *is* a limey!'

Horse's bulk shook gently with silent laughter.

I was perplexed. 'What do you mean?'

'You said "God save the Queen",' Horse attempted to explain. 'That sure as hell means you're a limey.' They both rocked with laughter for a while, leaving me just as confused.

Horse then addressed the matter in hand, nudging one of the tequila glasses in front of me. 'Here's what you do.' With a slow exaggerated motion he licked the saddle of his thumb, sprinkled salt on it, then lifted the tequila to his lips. It was a faintly golden liquid, and he poured it in slowly, evidently enjoying it, free of all desire to rush it. He set the empty glass down, let out an appreciative 'Ah!' and said, 'Then, if you like, you can do the other stuff.' He licked the salt, with one big slow slurp of his tongue, and bit on the lime.

'So there you go. All yours.' He handed me the salt-shaker. Something about the way he had taken the drink had already mesmerized me. I had never seen anyone drink tequila so slowly, and with such evident pleasure. My experience of it had always been a rushed, urgent one, with the salt and lime used as quickly as possible in order to get rid of the taste. But now, dimly aware of some distant sense of guilt, I decided to try it his way, unhurriedly. Sure enough, it did taste good – a slightly sweet, quite viscous fluid, warming in the chest, not burning.

Horse raised his eyebrows after I had done the salt and lime at the same measured pace. 'What say you, limey?'

'Excellent.'

The word elicited more guffaws.

'See that?' Dean said, gesturing at the wall behind the bar. Instead of the usual mirror, an array of postcard-sized squares of wood covered it, each one bearing an unintelligible symbol, a black glyph. I had been wondering what they were, and asked Dean now. 'Down in your left-hand corner,' he replied.

In the bottom left, just above a dusty, unopened bottle of crème de menthe, hung one of the varnished little boards, on which an upside-down 'Y' had been inscribed, with a dot either side of the letter's stem.

'That's Hoss's,' he said.

'Horse's what?'

'Horse's brand. That whole wall there's all brands. All of Tularosa and the Black Range, every ranch is up there.'

'And what's that?' I asked, pointing out a card I had noticed on which was printed a puzzling series of random capital letters. I wondered if it might also somehow be related to ranching.

A curious smile appeared on Dean's lips. He leant against the bar, his back to the wall, and began to recite a list of letters. I studied the card, and realized he was telling off the same list, but without looking at it. He knew it by heart.

'How did I do?'

'Just fine,' Horse said.

'What is it?' I asked again.

Horse let out a low snigger. Dean smirked at me, took a pull on his Coors Lite. 'That? Just a little something it's good to know.' They glanced at each other. Then Horse said, 'Nah,' with a kind of breadth in his voice, 'That's just – well, they changed the law here, and now the bar staff are supposed to check for DWIs' – driving while under the influence – 'and if you can't read off those letters they won't let you go. Have to pay for a cab home.' He shook his head. 'So it's good to learn those damn letters. Eighty miles of cab is no joke.'

'You live eighty miles away?'

He nodded. 'Sure. It's nothing in your own truck. But it's a long way at upwards of a dollar a mile.'

Just then the lights in the whole place flickered on and off. I looked around, but everyone carried on dancing and drinking, just as before. Then it happened again, a moment later.

'Here we go,' Dean said. 'Guess that's my call.' He tipped up his beer and let it all drain into his throat in one frothy surge.

'Wait a minute, wait a minute,' Horse restrained him. 'Show him your thing there.'

Without a moment's hesitation Dean undid his belt and detached the buckle. For an instant it crossed my mind that the bar was just about crowded enough for some bizarre drunken pervert to attempt some strange kind of assault without fear of being noticed, and I took half a step back as Dean reached out to show me the great buckle. It had a picture of a bull embossed on the bronze, and the word 'Champion' below it.

'I'm a healer,' Dean explained.

'A what?' I wondered if perhaps he meant some kind of cattle medicine-man.

'He ropes by the hind legs,' Horse clarified. 'They call it heelin'. He's a heeler. And that ain't all he does. You wait.'

Dean vanished into the crowd, and once more the lights flickered, only this time they stayed off. The band finished its song and the vocalist announced, in the darkness: 'We're takin' a break now and you all's in for a fun-packed time.'

No sooner had he switched off his mike than bright lights suddenly flooded the other end of the building. Dolly appeared from somewhere and grabbed my hand. 'Come on,' she said, and pulled me off through the crowd towards the lights.

'What's going on?'

'It's the rodeo,' she said.

Sure enough, up at the other end of the hall waited a sand pit enclosed by iron bars. People gathered round the cage and soon surrounded it. A gate stood closed at the far side, and it was a moment before I realized that through its railings I was staring at the black faces of two bulls. They seemed incongruous, hopelessly out of place, and their wide, round eyes looked lost and bewildered. Beyond them, outside, was the desert night.

The first bull was led by a nose-rope into a narrow pen, where a cowboy reached down to tie a long rope round its belly, from which hung a cow-bell, apparently there to irritate the animal. Then the first rider, a man in white chaps and hat, climbed off a fence directly onto the bull's back, where he gently settled himself on the beast. Meanwhile, three men were waiting in the sand pit: one who held the first gate shut, another to open the second gate with a rope once the rider was thrown, and a third, the clown, who had draped himself with long, coloured handkerchiefs and wore a big Mexican hat, braces, and eye-catching trinkets. His job was to distract the bull and lure it towards the second gate and out of the pen.

The rider whooped. The first man pulled the gate open. The bull jumped out, kicking its legs high. The fat muscles on its rump bulged and flexed. It snorted, its eyes the size of tennis balls. The clown waved and yahooed, skipping backwards over the sand, while the cowboy clung on for two or three buckings, leaning right back, then fell off. He scrambled out of the way in the soft sand, while the bull kicked and bucked furiously around the ring, until the clown led it to the far gate, where the animal spotted its escape and calmly trotted out.

Immediately the process started again with the next bull. There were six bulls that night, like a bullfight, and on the back of the fourth rode Dean. But he was apparently better at heeling bulls than riding them. He didn't last more than a second, but to make up for his humiliatingly short ride he stood in the ring brushing the sand off his sleeves and trousers while the bull kicked its way towards the dancing, skipping clown, and finally out of the gate.

As soon as the gate closed on the sixth bull the lights went out on the rodeo and the band struck up again.

I turned round to find Dolly gone. The crowd had thinned towards the end of the rodeo, as the cowboys found more important things to do, and she had apparently drifted off too, or else been swept off. I walked the length of the place and eventually spotted her up by the bar, laughing beneath a cluster of five stetsons. I decided not to interrupt, and wandered about half-heartedly looking for Charlie. Once I caught a glimpse of her among the two-steppers on the dance floor, her hair suddenly enflamed by a roaming spotlight.

We didn't leave till late. Dolly and Charlie both took me out for a second spin on the floor later on, out of politeness, and both said I was dancing much better now. But they had many suitors to attend to.

It was a while before Dean reappeared at the bar. Horse bought him a shot of Silver Herradura tequila and said, 'I ain't gonna ask.'

'Don't.'

'All right then. Just drink up and let's get out of here. You've got a long drive, Mr Taxicab.' They bought themselves another final round, and then another, and then left.

It was only when the band started packing up their equipment that Dolly finally said, 'Oh well, I guess we better call it a night.'

'What a night,' echoed Charlie.

They both fell asleep on the drive home.

THREE

A Priest with No Name

THE NEXT DAY was a bad day. It was overcast right through till nightfall, when a few stars appeared for a minute then vanished again. It drizzled all morning, a fine veil-like drizzle which seemed negligible but drenched me when I strolled across the meadow. The countryside was dismal in the rain. I remembered how dreary mountains can be in bad weather.

Dolly took me to a community cook-out in Bakersville, ten miles to the east. Because of the rain the event was taking place in a classroom at the local high school. Pots of spare ribs, chilli con carne and coleslaw stood on a line of school desks, from behind which large smiling women served up paper plates of the food. You could buy beers and sodas at another table. After lunch there was an auction to raise money for the school. A can of Budweiser went for thirty-five dollars.

A lanky cowboy in a stetson talked to Dolly and me about the 'niggers' running the country in Washington. He made a point of glancing back over his shoulder just before he said the word each time, then leaned conspiratorially towards us with a sly smile. 'I had to call them niggers four times to straighten out my social security payments,' he told us. 'Who's running the country anyway?'

Dolly beamed at him throughout, her faith in cowboys unshaken.

In the middle of the afternoon, while I was reading in the trailer, feeling somewhat deflated after the thrills of the previous night, there was a light tap on the door.

It was Dolly. 'Excuse me,' she said, smoothing down her denim

34

skirt after taking two big steps up into the trailer. She sat on the sofa and rested her chin in her hands. 'I have to talk to you.'

'What is it?'

She cleared her throat and glanced out of the little window and told me that she and Gust, the friend who had given me her number, were lovers. She hadn't known that he was dating another woman. 'You see,' she concluded, 'although he's away a lot – at least that's what he said – I do have quite a liking for him. I *did*, anyways. Before all this.'

For some reason I felt guilty. Briefly, a beam of dread picked me out. I knew what was coming. She went on to say that she just couldn't get used to having me here. It wasn't my fault, but I had brought her bad news, and she needed some time. She had checked the buses and there was one leaving for Santa Fe and Taos at ten o'clock the next morning. She would be more than happy to run me down to Alamogordo to catch it. There was no need for me to take a taxi.

Oddly, I felt better at once. Taos was where I would go. Suddenly it seemed obvious to me that I wanted to move on. This was cowboy country, and what I had come for was Indian country, the Indian country up in the north of the state.

I packed my bag in anticipation and zipped it up, even though I knew I would only have to open it again later to get out my toothbrush.

The next morning we stopped in at Cooper's Western Warehouse on the way to the bus. I felt my pilgrimage beginning in earnest now, and decided that such a voyage required appropriate footwear. Obviously, the thing to have was a pair of cowboy boots, and Cooper's was the place for boots. I moved along the aisles, passing yard after yard of cowboy footwear – snakeskin, lizard skin, Justin Ropers, Cuban heels, black suede, brown suede, patent leather, rough inside-out leather – and finally selected a suede pair, and a straw stetson with a woven Indian band for Dolly. Then we cruised on to the Sonic Diner for a breakfast of chilli burgers and fries, which we ate from trays clipped on to the windows of the truck, squeezing sachets of vinegary mustard into the buns.

Dolly giggled and said, 'Well, it's not exactly a refined breakfast.'

'Mom. C'mon. It's the Sonic. What do you expect?'

'That's what I mean.' She coughed.

'Anyway, breakfast is never refined. Breakfast is just breakfast.' Dolly coughed again.

After we finished, I crumpled up all our papers, trying not to spill salt from the torn packets, and stuffed a great bundle of debris into a red bin outside. A fierce wind was blowing. Two napkins escaped from the load and fluttered away into the field behind the diner.

When I climbed back in Charlie was talking about recycling. 'Jesus,' she was saying, 'in Harlem they have garbage patrols now. They catch you with a can in your garbage, or a bottle, they fine you. It's about time, too. You think that'll ever catch on in Alamogordo? No, sir.'

'I was just saying that it's different out here. There's so much space, so much – I don't know, *country*. You can't hardly hurt it,' said Dolly.

Charlie rolled her eyes. Dolly was about to go on, but checked herself. She let out a polite laugh as I settled myself behind the wheel. She was wearing the hat I had bought for her, and adjusted the brim and flipped down the sun blind to look in the vanity mirror. 'I just love my hat,' she sang.

Charlie, who was seated in the back and apparently felt that some word of approval was called for, said, 'It's a good hat.'

I drove towards the Chevron gas station a mile up the street, where the bus stopped. Even down here on the desert in Alamogordo the weather was bleak. It was warm, but deeply overcast, and looked dark enough for a thunderstorm. The traffic lights which hung from wires above the road were tossing about in the wind. In front of a carpet store three flags were beating themselves about so loudly you could hear them inside the truck. Looking east I could see nothing of the mountains which rose up less than two miles away. They were lost in a wiry cloud. It seemed that the whole world was a flat, windy desert covered by seal-coloured clouds.

I wasn't surprised when a streak of lightning appeared right in front of us a mile down the road.

'Here we go,' Charlie said.

There was another flash off to the side, but no rain. We reached the Chevron and pulled in under the shelter to await the downpour. On the street the cars had switched on their headlamps. It was strange – the dark sky, the glare of the lights, the periodic flashes, but no rain and no thunder. Just a fierce wind. The truck jogged about as if a large man were leaning back against it and digging his heels in to rock it.

The bus arrived before the rain. Dolly and Charlene climbed out to say goodbye before I could tell them not to bother. Before she had even opened the back for my bag Dolly's new hat was tumbling past the petrol pumps. I ran after it, leaping faster than I expected, helped on by the wind. The hat disappeared under the bus. I went to the far side. There was no sign of it. I peered underneath, and saw it sitting the right way up under the middle of the bus. I swung my leg under and tried to hook it with the toe of my boot, but it was beyond my reach.

Meanwhile Charlie had given my bag to the blue-uniformed driver. He loaded it in the locker beneath the windows.

'I can't get it,' I told Dolly.

She smiled. 'I'll just wait till you-all are on your way.'

I offered to buy a ticket when I climbed on, but the driver wouldn't take my money. 'Wait till Tularosa,' he said. 'We got us our office there.' He was a middle-aged man with a black moustache and a ring of brush-like hair surrounding his bald pate, and spoke in a soft, clipped voice, lingering on the sibilants. He snorted through his nose as he reached for the steel handle that closed the door.

We pulled out to the edge of the forecourt. I looked back. Dolly was holding her hat onto her head and stalking her way back to the Ram Charger, leaning forwards. Charlene was already behind the wheel.

I waved. Dolly saw and sent me an awkward farewell with her left arm. Charlene switched the headlights on and off and then on again. I thought I saw her waving behind the reflections on the windshield.

The bus growled dully, and I felt two bumps as we turned out into the traffic, pointing north. We were on the road.

The humming monotony of the straight road soon lulled me into reveries. I found myself recalling my early intimations of a New Mexican soujourn.

The first piece of mail I ever received came from New Mexico. It arrived one morning soon after I learnt to buckle my shoes. I was busy fitting the prong into the hole when my mother called up the stairwell: 'There's something for you, darling.'

I ran down the stairs with my shoes flapping. My mother was in the kitchen, a big room with a long window and a thick wood table.

'Mum,' I cried.

She was pouring from the kettle into a pan. A cloud of steam swirled up bright into the sunlight.

'Look by the front door.'

I went into the hall. There was nothing there, just some letters lying on the floor like every morning. I was puzzled. Then it dawned on me. Someone had sent me a letter. It must have been my father, who was away teaching at the University of New Mexico. I dropped to my knees and rummaged through the pile. A blue corner appeared. I pulled out a postcard, a glossy picture of a funfair with red hills in the background and a deep blue sky. I turned it over.

There, in block letters, it said: 'HENRY.'

My father had printed out a message for me. 'It is hot here. The

sun shines all day. There are big red mountains. I miss you.'
At the bottom it said, 'LOVE, DAD.'

I read it twice kneeling there on the floor, ran into the kitchen
and read it again under the window and finally asked my mother:
'Where's it from? Where is Dad?'

'He's in Albuquerque,' she said. 'It's come all the way from
Albuquerque.'

'Where's that?'

'It's in America.' She was lifting an egg out of the pan. She put
it gently in an egg cup and tapped it with the back of a spoon.

'America?' I liked saying the word.

'Yes. In New Mexico.' She put the eggs on the table then stooped
to fasten my shoes for me.

'New Mexico? Is that in America too?'

Albuquerque. New Mexico. America. There was something
about the words – they all had it – something unutterably exotic.
It was as if the words themselves had flown all the way from there,
from a place where life was quite different and very lovely. I fell in
love with them.

My father got back two months later. He brought me a black
plastic submarine a yard long.

'Did you get it in Albuquerque? In a toy shop?'

'Yes.' He chuckled. 'In a store in Albuquerque. They call shops
stores in America.'

The submarine came with a little canister of pills. You opened
the turret and put a pill inside and swung it shut again, then when
you put the submarine under water in the bath it blew a chain of
little silver bubbles out of the turret. They looked like the plug
chain. After every bath I dried it in a towel and put it at the back
of my cupboard. I stood the silver canister beside it. It was my
best toy.

Twelve years later, when I went to Cambridge, I read about New
Mexico. My first digs were in a house owned by an alcoholic

computer programmer who used to disappear into her bedroom for days on end with cases of wine. During her retreats I would hear her groan, sniff, and sometimes knock things over. Occasionally she would emerge, her face mottled, the hair glued to her forehead, and stumble into the bathroom.

She rented her other spare room to a forty-year-old man who had long ago been a student at Cambridge, and had never left. He washed dishes in the kitchen of his former college now, and in his spare time drank beer in pubs and read fiction. He used to invite me into his den when he got back from the pub, and read out excerpts from *Under the Volcano*, his favourite novel. He would pause every few sentences to top up the whisky in his late-night coffee, making it a progressively thinner excuse, until eventually his reading became indistinct.

His collection of books had spread throughout the house. They filled two walls of shelves in my room and were piled high against a third. I used to pluck titles at random out of the stacks. One Tuesday afternoon when it was already dark outside, and raining, I came in and slumped onto the bed in my damp overcoat. I reached up behind my head and pulled down an old hardback. It had a red cover and the spine was so faded that you couldn't make out the title. It was a lightweight book, an edition from some publisher's popular library. I opened it in the middle and sneezed.

> . . . which I am I, after all, now that I have drunk a glass to
> St Catherine, and the moon shines over the sea, and my
> thoughts must needs follow the moon-track south-west, to the
> great South-west, where the ranch is . . .

I recognized the cadence of Lawrence's prose right away, and flicked through the pages, jumping from passage to passage, plunging straight in each time.

> . . . my little ranch, and the three horses down among the
> timber . . . the moon shines on the alfalfa slope, between the
> pines, and the cabins are blind . . . Only the big pine tree in
> front of the house, standing still and unconcerned, alive . . .

As I read my heart began to race. I became hot and tugged at my sleeves to pull off the heavy coat. I felt myself blush. The words seemed to rise a quarter of an inch clear of the paper. I could hardly believe what I was reading.

> . . . Italy, so reputedly old, yet for ever so child-like and naive! Never, never for a moment able to comprehend the wonderful, hoary age of America, the continent of the afterwards . . . In a cold like this, the stars snap like distant coyotes, beyond the moon. And the place heaves with ghosts . . . Away beyond is a light, at Taos, or at Ranchos de Taos, a ruddy point of human light . . .

New Mexico, pine trees, mountains, moonlight, a ranch, the hoary age of America – I had the strange feeling that I was reading about my own life. This was the very life that suited me, that was waiting for me. Suddenly I realized I wanted it very badly. It was as if I had been waiting for it, but I didn't need to any more. Right now I was ready, I wanted to be there, up a mountainside overlooking the desert of New Mexico. I could already see it in the early morning, stretching away smooth and pale, with red hills in the distance. My body seemed to change subtly. It was as if all the arteries expanded and the blood flowed more freely, and my joints became loose, freshly oiled.

Which I am I? The question seemed to run through my entire frame. For three weeks now I had been putting off writing an essay on Homer. I had been spending the days tramping from library to library, stopping off for coffee between them. In the libraries I would open a book, read a sentence and start to daydream. Hours would slip by as I stared at the windows, too high to see anything out of except the eraser-smudged sky – they built them high like in Victorian schools so you wouldn't get distracted – when I could be vibrant and alive, feeling packed full of life, and living somewhere I wanted, doing something I wanted.

I sat down at the table in my room, slouched on my elbows and heard a thump overhead: the landlady knocking something over.

My essay was due the next day. I reached for the plastic bag that was doing service as briefcase, touched it and drew my hand back. Which I am I? America was actually there, on the other side of the globe: the continent of the afterwards. I wasn't exactly sure what Lawrence meant by that, but it sounded good. And somewhere in the deserts of America the rooftops of Albuquerque were glittering like a jewel, right now.

I walked to the window. It was black night outside. The back windows of the neighbourhood shed streaks of light here and there among the bare twigs and branches. It was raining softly. I saw it flashing in the halo of a back-door light. It had been raining like that for two days.

There were only three other people on the bus, a large young Hispanic lady sitting up at the front, and two men in jeans and T-shirts with short haircuts and clipped moustaches, who looked like they could have been on leave from the Mexican army. I rested my temple against the vibrating window and watched the sagging telegraph lines flick upwards each time a pole went by.

Somewhere we passed a road sign that listed various destinations. At the bottom was Carrizozo, 128 miles. Carrizozo was where the Flying Father who used to visit the airport in Vermont came from. I remembered the name of his home town clearly, and found myself falling into a daydream about him now. I remembered his sleek plane and the way he slid back the roof of his cockpit right after he landed, and shouted to me over the bleating of the dying engine to fill it up. I wondered what had happened to him, if he still flew to Vermont once a month and lived in New Mexico. I felt strangely dislocated. Alone on a bus seven years after all that, gurgling towards the Flying Father's town, looking for something I couldn't name. It made me lonely for a second. And then happy. For one thing, I realized that I was on a search, and that whatever it was, it was bigger than my ill-starred relationship with Frankie had been. This mattered more than that had done. It seemed good to be out here alone on a bus, roaming across the parched, wintry-looking land.

I found myself thinking about Joel the sculptor too. I wondered if he was still in New Mexico, still making things he liked, and if he still cropped his hair. It was odd, but thinking of him, and of the Flying Father, made me feel like I had friends out here, like these two men were part of a gang that included me now. They didn't know I was here, and they probably never would know, but I felt that they would be pleased if they did.

The bus went on, its engine grinding away beneath the floor, steadily creeping up the Tularosa Basin, the two mountain ranges on either side just visible on the horizons, one smooth and faint and green, the other jagged, crystalline, blue. In another four hours it would growl into Taos, way up in the north of the state.

Before lunch we crossed a ridge of little hills and drove into a small storm. For five minutes the rain obscured everything. Then we came down the far side between trailer homes bristling with television aerials, with washing lines laced between them from which hung limp, translucent clothes. I looked up and saw, high above, blue cliffs cracked like dried-out dough. Mesquite trees clung to them, sprouting from the crevices. A hill sat brooding under a cloud with its paws in the sunshine. The tatters of the storm were strewn across the sky like an old tapestry. It was the end of the overcast weather.

A sign by the roadside flashed by. 'Rain for Rent,' it declared, without explanation.

Carrizozo stepped closer with each road sign. Soon we passed a billboard saying 'Zozo Welcomes You', and rolled into a set of low concrete houses on the edge of the town, then on to a strip of old motels. We stopped outside the 4 Winds Restaurant. 'Twenty minutes,' the driver called.

Inside, everything belonged to the Willy Loman era: self-stirring fish-tanks of Vitality Brand orange juice, big old sugar shakers with flaps over the spout, red plastic beakers for water. The menu said: 'Warning!!! Our chief cook has determined that eating our Mexican food is potentially habit forming.' Outside the window I could see the signs of motels called Sunset and Siesta and Desert Sands.

Four workers in blue shirts, all Hispanic, were eating silently under the long front window, methodically spooning a red stew into their mouths with their eyes fixed on the bowls in front of them. Now and then one of them put down his spoon, wiped his mouth and took a swig from a red glass of iced water, gazing about the room briefly, seeing nothing. I wasn't hungry, but I ordered a burrito anyway, then waited, listening to the sound of the waitress emptying used plates into a plastic bin, and a radio in the kitchen, on which a man was singing a mournful Mexican ballad to the accompaniment of wailing trumpets.

While I waited I found myself thinking about the Flying Father. I was more and more curious about him. I remembered how I had admired his life, his freedom, his mission. I realized I wanted to try to see him. Here I was in his very town.

I caught the waitress as she was going by with a stack of dirty plates.

'Is there a church around?' I asked.

She was a plump young woman, and was wearing too much lipstick. 'A church?' She said it quietly, neatly, the word coming out like a little brick. 'Sure. Just along a ways on your left hand.'

The twenty minutes of our stop were ticking by. Finally I could wait no longer. Before the food came I got up, leaving a five-dollar bill to cover my check plus a large tip, and opened the door.

It was quiet and still outside, not a breath of wind. A high, clear, singing sky. I passed the Sunset Motel, with a sign outside on which big black plastic letters had been affixed: 'New Mattesse,' it advertised. The final 's' was hanging upside down, caught by the pin at the bottom. It looked like it had been hanging that way a long time.

The church stood next door, a simple wooden hut painted red

with a tin roof. An all-purpose sign similar to the motel's stood at the roadside. 'Carrizozo Reform Baptist Church,' it said. It gave the times of the services and the name of the Pastor: Ray Wilson.

I couldn't remember the Flying Father's name, if I had ever known it, but I doubted that was it. He also hadn't seemed like a Baptist. My plan was to find out which was his church from any local priest I ran into, and then see if there was time to get over there before the bus left. Or else see if I could catch a later bus. But the church was all locked up and there was no one around. I stood on tiptoe to peer through a window. It was dark inside and I could barely make out the rows of benches. I turned back to the road, feeling a little frustrated, apparently wanting to see him more strongly than I had realized. It was sad to be stymied so quickly.

Just then a sky-blue wood-trimmed Plymouth station-wagon pulled in to the kerb. A woman with spiky blonde hair and a big diamond on her steering-wheel hand buzzed down the window. 'You look like you need help. You looking for anyone? We mostly don't meet up but on Sundays.' She added that they had a Wednesday prayer meeting to which I would be very welcome. That was in two days' time.

I thanked her, and explained what I was looking for.

'A priest with no name, huh? But he flies planes?' She chuckled. 'Well, a number of them do. What church would he be?'

I shrugged, and tried describing him.

A smile broke out on her face. She nodded. 'Uh-huh.' She seemed to find it amusing. 'I think you're talking about Padre Bertoni.'

'Bertoni?' It sounded Italian. I thought about it and decided that the Flying Father could indeed have been of Italian extraction. There was a certain sharpness, a brusque yet stylish efficiency about him.

'Mm-huh,' she went on. 'Yup. He moved. They sent him on up to Las Vegas, I believe.'

'Las Vegas?' So that was that, I thought. Vegas was states away.

'Yup. You go up to Santa Fe and make a dog-leg over thataways.' She yanked her thumb towards the motel opposite.

'It's in Nevada, right?'

She shook her head. 'That's *the* Vegas. This is Las Vegas, New Mexico. You can hike it over from Santa Fe, or you can double back down to it from Taos.'

'Las Vegas, New Mexico,' I repeated. 'Thank you.'

'You'll find old Bertoni there.'

I ran back to the restaurant, suddenly worried about missing the bus, which I could see parked ahead, expecting any moment to see a flurry of black smoke blow from the back. But when I reached it the driver was just opening up the door. I glanced through the window into the restaurant. The waitress was setting out fresh covers at an empty table. She glanced up and frowned at me, raising the cloth in her hand in a shrug, then sent me a big, red smile.

Far away, sixty miles away, a silhouette of blue mountains sat on the horizon, delicate like sea-haze, or like the fin of a fish, or like an insect wing. It was a perfect, clear day now. The only vestige of the morning's weather was a fleet of little puffs of steam that drifted above the ground like wisps of a morning mist, high miniature clouds grazing the hills.

We climbed into a landscape of red undulations studded with piñon bushes, motionless under a dark blue sky. A billboard suddenly declared, in big, swirly writing: 'Santa Fe. 30 Miles. 56 Hotels. 26 Motels. 107 Restaurants.'

Across the plain stretched the road, dead straight, receding into the bulk of blue mountains ahead like tape feeding into a machine. Those far mountains, a single body like a castle, with the highway its drawbridge, were the Sangre de Cristos Mountains. At their feet huddled the far-flung outpost of New Spain, the lonely capital Santa Fe, city of the holy faith.

The fifty-six hotels scared me. I had thought Santa Fe was a quiet

town of fifty thousand inhabitants. I was glad my ticket said Taos
on it.

In fact I liked everything about my bus ticket. Instead of being
a scroll of thin paper, like an English one, it was a stiff card the size
of a postcard. It said: 'TNMO' – Texas, New Mexico, Oklahoma –
which was the name of the local Greyhound company, then, just
below: 'Destination – Taos'. And beneath that: 'Boarding point –
Alamogordo'. There were some rules about smoking and drinking
and personal stereos on the back. It was a well-made object. It
would make a good souvenir. I felt like writing an address on it
and mailing it to a friend with my news scribbled in the margin.

We reached a great plateau, suede-like, smoothed to khaki in the
distance as if grazed by sheep. In the middle ran a smoky gash, the
canyon of the Rio Grande, and to the side stood a clump of tremendous purple and white mountains. It was only four in the afternoon
but clouds were brooding above the peaks, and in the little town
of Taos at their foot lights had been lit. Those little pricks of light
made the town unbearably welcoming and remote. They made the
landscape enormous: the wide plain of sagebrush, the mesa, a flat
tableland lifting away to the west, and the other way the impossibly
dark mountains. It all seemed mythical and vast, belonging to some
other world. It was as if the scene stretched some rarely used muscle
of the imagination.

It was confusing. Suddenly it seemed possible that when I rode
into that little cluster of houses and lights bedded up against the
bulk of mountain my life would never be the same again.

Taos stands at seven thousand feet in the middle of a desert, an
ideal climate for consumptives. It occurred to me as I stepped out
of the bus and smelt the faintly dusty air of a high desert, sneezing
at the arid cleanness, that D. H. Lawrence might have come here
for the climate. New Mexico, Vence, the Australian desert: it was
possible that his 'savage pilgrimage', his years of wandering with
his wife Frieda in search of a powerful, elemental culture, had in

47

fact been a quest for a climate that would give him a few more years of life. Lawrence was a sick man, but he spent his life feverishly espousing a Nietzschean philosophy of rude health. It was the philosophy of an invalid, I now saw. For the first time I felt sorry for him. I had the sensation, as I glanced across the green sage-covered desert reaching away to the horizon, that life was simpler, more attainable, more accessible in every way than it normally seemed. Lawrence was no saint, but an uneasy sick man with an eye to his public image. He wasn't in essence different from anybody else. He had been to New Mexico, and now so had I, and so had countless others. It was simple: if you wanted to go to New Mexico all you had to do was go. It required no special permission.

I felt free, and for a moment everything in life seemed small and easy to shift about, as if all my desires and efforts were toys made of cardboard and balsa wood, like the stations and garages of a toy train set. You could pick them up and move them about as easily as you could sneeze. It was as if we were all giants pretending to be dwarfed by the miniature streets we designed for ourselves to walk along. In reality we could just as easily step between them, go where we liked.

And it was warm out. The air felt good. Air that suits the tubercular suits anyone. It was balm.

FOUR

The Cheapest Motel on the Mesa

I FOUND MYSELF at another Chevron gas station. I went into the shop and poured myself a foam cup of coffee from the machine by the window, then browsed the aisles in search of nourishment. My new boots clicked enjoyably on the linoleum, and I could feel their shafts holding and protecting my calves. I narrowed down my choice of food to Oreo cookies or tortilla chips, and scanned the jars of salsa for the mildest one.

A large Indian woman sat at the cash register, dressed in the stiff red uniform of the gas station. I asked her how I could get into town. Outside I could see a motel across the highway, then the plain stretching to the horizon.

'Town? We're in town.'

'What about the plaza?' I had read about Taos's famous plaza and as far as I could see we were in the middle of an empty land.

'What about it?' She spoke in a soft, but rhythmic, accented voice. It was a soothing speech to hear.

'Where is it? Is there any way of getting to it?'

'Sure. You go straight down 68 till you hit the lights in town.'

That sounded like what I needed: traffic lights, a junction, the plaza – it surely added up to a town centre. But I had yet to come to grips with the West, to which the very notion of a centre is antithetical. The settling of the West was the story of a flight from all centres.

'But how can I get to it? Is there a bus?'

She stared at me. 'The only bus is the TNMO. I guess the driver

49

wouldn't take you but three miles down the road.' She shrugged her shoulders. 'You could ask him though. But he won't be coming through till four o'clock.'

'Four o'clock?' I could see the clock behind her head. It was four twenty.

'Yeah, he just went by. The next bus is four o'clock. Tomorrow, that is.' She was silent a moment. 'You mean you don't have a car?'

'I came on the bus.'

'You coulda asked him to drop youse in town.' She shrugged. 'I guess you better call up Frank.'

'Frank?'

'Frank's Limousine Service. He might come for you.'

The company card was taped to the telephone.

'How manys are you?' a male voice barked on the other end.

'One,' I said. 'I think.'

A woman stood outside in the forecourt in a red anorak beside a row of suitcases. 'Maybe two. I see someone else waiting outside.'

'Where are you going?'

'Town.'

'Where?'

'The plaza. The traffic lights.'

'The what?'

'Just the middle, the middle of town.'

He paused. 'No hotel? No home? Nothing? Well, OK,' he sang.

Just then a red Nissan Pathfinder covered in dust swooped onto the forecourt. A man in jeans and a denim shirt opened up the back, kissed the woman waiting and picked up her bags.

The Chevron was right on the edge of town, four miles from the plaza. I climbed into Frank's dark grey station-wagon, with 'Frank's Service' emblazoned on its doors, and watched large low stores spaced out along the highway pass by. A jeans warehouse, a paint store, a couple of motels. It was all a bleak and barren scene in the cloudy afternoon. Yet I felt only a warm curiosity. I liked the dismal scene.

I asked the driver if there was a cheap hotel in town.

'Cheap? As in no caro? We just passed the Sand Chateau, cheapest motel on the mesa.'

We were still evidently some way from the real town, too far for me. I wanted to be in the cheap, old part of it. This was Spanish America, and Taos, being a Spanish town, would surely have a cheap, old centre.

'What about in town?'

'What is it with the town? We're in town. This is town.'

I glanced out at the mesa, empty, flat, pale green, at the highway and the double telegraph poles like staples stitching the road to the plain, and at the two lines of low businesses set back either side of the road. It struck me then that this was the very fringe of Spanish America. This was its furthest reach, its frontier. It gave me a sudden brief sense of achievement to be here.

'You wanna go out of town you go up into the mountains. Or onto the mesa.'

'The plaza,' I said. 'Just the plaza. That'll be fine.' I was getting a little nervous now. I didn't fancy traipsing up this highway on foot with my bag over my shoulder trying to find a room in a motel. This was not a place for pedestrians. I imagined night falling while I was still patrolling the verges, with the headlights flashing by in the dark.

The driver braked suddenly as a cop car swerved into our lane and switched on its siren. The wail lifted slowly like a yawn, and the car drew away, accelerating with the bulky smoothness of a big speedboat in a bay. We hung back. Once we steadied out again I pursued my interrogation about the hotels.

'You've got the bed and breakfasts,' he said. 'There's a couple of them. But cheap? I don't know. You can't beat the Sand Chateau. Like I said.'

The road rose up ahead between a cluster of adobe buildings. They were clean and new-looking and a sidewalk ran along beside them.

'You tell me where,' the driver said, running the back of a finger along his moustache.

'The plaza,' I repeated.

We passed a store selling cowboy boots and moccasins, then one called 'Seven Thousand T-Shirts', its name glowing in green neon. It made me think of the T-shirt Frankie had given me. Perhaps she had bought it in that very store. It almost gave me a shock to think of it. I let out an involuntary sigh. Perhaps I had finally come to the origin of that shirt. Right here was where its life began.

The shops were open on the plaza, and the parking meters around the square were all taken, but there were no people to be seen. I strolled through the lanes and streets: they were all quiet. In front of the Plaza Bakery, which stood by a parking lot nearby, a hippie family were seated on the pavement with various wares spread before them on a shawl. The father was a wiry man with grey hair and a Navajo headband. He was selling a set of ceramic pots he had made. They all had fine black lines fired into their glaze.

'Hair,' he told me. 'I use hair.'

He spoke in a soft, wavering voice.

'Your own?'

He chuckled, but with just a hint of precariousness, as if any second he might fall into uncontrollable hysterics. 'Any hair I can get.' He shrugged and snickered again. He was sitting with his knees pulled into his chest.

His wife had long black hair partly tied into a ponytail, partly fanning out about her sun-tanned face. Hers was stiff, wiry hair. I wondered if it would be good for his glazes. She was wearing a long lilac cotton dress and no shoes.

I asked where they lived.

'In the Kit Carson National Forest,' she said, speaking in the same soft, clipped voice I had heard all day. It seemed to be the New Mexico accent.

'What's that? Just forest?'

'Oh, forests, mountains, rivers, lakes,' she said airily. 'We've got all kinds there.' Then she laughed, too.

'What's your place like?'

'It's just a place. A wood house.'

'Does it have water and electricity?'

'Jake brought us a solar unit but it's not working. But we got plenty of water. There's a stream right by us.' The word sounded like *strim*.

'You wash in the stream?'

'Of course,' she sang. 'We make candles too, and we cook on the fire and sometimes we make a big fire and do a sweat.'

'A sweat?'

'A sweat lodge. To get real squeaky clean,' she laughed.

'Why don't you come out with us,' the third family member piped up. She was a girl of about fourteen, plump, draped in a baggy white dress with a blue and silver shawl over her shoulders. She had glitter makeup on her cheeks and in her hair. She was staring at me, her mouth open. 'Don't ask all those questions, come and visit,' she repeated.

She had a shiny dark face and big lips. Her black hair was tousled and along with the glitter I saw little pieces of hay in it. She seemed feral, like the untamed wolf-boy in the Mad Max films. She got up, all the while staring at me, and came over to me. She touched my forearm and said, 'I like you. I want you to come out to the National Forest. You never seen anything like it. Trees, trees, trees.'

'When are you going?'

'Soon, soon. As soon as Grey sells a pot. Or maybe he won't sell a pot and we'll go anyway. Do you want to buy a pot?'

'They're nice but I haven't got enough money.' He was asking sixty dollars for the smallest one, which was the size of a teacup.

'Maybe next time,' the mother said. She had apparently been listening to our exchange.

'Yes.'

'If Courtenay wants you to come visit you're very welcome,' she added.

'Oh, yes, yes,' the girl repeated.

All kinds of things flashed through my mind. The girl was definitely post-pubescent. She had a sizable bust to prove it. But when she said she liked me, what did she mean? And did it matter anyway? And was she mildly demented, or was this a truly natural human being, the like of which I had never met before? Were these very doubts of mine, these hedgings and questionings, the inhibited response of an over-civilized man? Should I be able to go along easily with this new situation that had presented itself, just as she was doing?

I asked, 'Have you got running water?'

'The stream is running,' the mother said. She paused.

'I mean in the house.' It must have sounded like I was trying to size up the likely accommodation, though in fact I was just curious about how they lived.

She smiled. 'Oh no. We don't need it. The house is right by the stream. When you have running water you get lots of other running things, too.' She snickered. 'Running worries, running troubles. Better not touch the system at all.'

I nodded, thinking smugly to myself that all hippies were paranoid. Her husband, the sheepish ceramicist who sat there on the ground strangely hunched behind his wares, was probably the victim of some drug turn that had gone wrong. The two of them probably lived out in the bush because they couldn't handle life anywhere else. I realized I was effectively dismissing them as write-offs, and was doing it with a somewhat malicious inner glee, yet I also couldn't deny a feeling of comfort I had around them. Something about them seemed to suit me. It worried me. It made me think that my condemnation must be dishonest, even desperate, an attempt to suppress a part of myself, but I didn't want to speculate what that part might be.

I checked over the notice-board in the bakery. It was a moment before I noticed Courtenay, the daughter, at my elbow. I felt I should say something to her, when I stopped myself. She was happy to stand there silently. Why shouldn't I? We scanned the notices together. There were ads for old cookers and mountain bikes and tents, Chevrolets, Dodges, Nissans and Hondas, and many house-shares. 'Non-smoking woman,' most of them required, which ruled me out twice. One little blue card, a formal-looking business card, advertised short-term rentals in small, comfortable adobes. Studios, one-bedrooms, two-bedrooms. There was a telephone number.

Courtenay tagged along when I went to the telephone. The woman who answered gave me directions. It was nearby. She had an adobe studio with a fireplace for eighty dollars a week. It sounded perfect.

I said goodbye to Courtenay. She didn't reply, but watched me walk across the parking lot. I glanced back from the far side. She was still staring at me, making me wonder again if I had been right about the dementedness.

I walked down Kit Carson Street, lined with swirling Gaudiesque adobe shops and art galleries. There were clothes boutiques and an antiquarian book-dealer and a regular bookstore with a café. It seemed strange. It was just a small street in a small town. The row of shops wasn't more than two hundred yards long, and it represented a good part of all the shops in town. Yet most of them were luxury stores. And there didn't seem to be any shoppers around, let alone anyone to buy old books of Audubon prints or five-thousand-dollar paintings. It puzzled me. The whole atmo-sphere of the place puzzled me. It was a quiet adobe town; and yet there was an air of self-assurance, a poise in the air, that you nor-mally find only in a city. It seemed a sophisticated, self-possessed little town.

The woman on the telephone was already parked in the com-pound, among the bare flaking trunks of a stand of eucalyptus. She was sitting in her white Honda with the engine running. As I lumbered into the gravel yard the motor stopped.

55

We shook hands. She had short black hair, a bulbous nose, and large turquoise Navajo earrings. 'This is it,' she said, unlocking a door.

There was a faintly musty smell, as if no one had stayed in it for a while. A thick carpet covered the floor, the bed was tucked into an alcove, and otherwise it was furnished with a new round table of pale pine, a sofa with a coffee table in front, and a TV. There was a kitchen and a bathroom and, in the far corner, the kiva fireplace, a smoothly moulded arch set in the whitewashed plaster. The room was dark and new, and three of the windows wouldn't open, but I liked it.

'I'll get the janitor,' she offered. 'He'll knock the windows open.'

'Any deals?' I asked, and immediately regretted saying it. It seemed like a fair deal already.

She smiled, hummed, looked out of the nearest window, one which I had managed to open. You could hear the eucalyptus leaves hissing high up.

'Seventy-five,' she said. 'My last offer. And when you leave, I'll throw in a free lift to the bus. You should have told me you didn't have a car.' For some reason we both chuckled.

I set about unpacking. I checked all the utensils in the kitchen, the linen and towels, and shortly before dusk went on my first shopping expedition in Taos. I came back with cans of bean soup, tortilla chips, and a bag of cedar logs for the fire. It was dark outside when I settled in front of the yellow, incense-rich flames with a bowl of soup.

As I brought the first spoon to my mouth I stopped and said a word by way of grace, and to remind myself: Taos.

FIVE

Sunshine Tree

TAOS WAS A SMALL TOWN, a good place to walk around. It had the remote, lucid feel of a mountain town, but also the arid smoothness of a desert town. I did all my shopping on foot. Every time I walked out my door and ambled along the road towards the plaza, I saw the purple and khaki mountains up on one side, and, from the rise in the road beside the first junction, the copper-green mesa stretching away flat to the west. They were good views, calming and big enough to occupy the vision. The mountains were like an absorbing painting thrust right up close. You couldn't help exploring their lines and shapes. Your mind changed to a slower gear, as if settling down in a comfortable armchair to examine the spectacle properly.

Strange things happened on my shopping trips. Every day in the afternoon I walked out of the compound and along Kit Carson Street, then crossed a plank over a ditch and threaded my way through a field, endeavouring not to get side-tracked on any of the deer paths in the dry grass. At the far side you had to jump over another ditch, then step up into a dusty carpark with a bank and a burger joint on either side. Opposite was Smith's Supermarket. Once, on my way home, I emerged from the ditch behind the parking lot to find a circle of ten Indian men seated in the long grass. They were chanting, but in such deep, rhythmic voices that it was a moment before I realized that the guttural murmuring I could hear was coming from them. It almost seemed to be a natural phenomenon, part of the surroundings. One man had a drum which he beat irregularly. They were all wearing jeans and cowboy boots, ponytails and T-shirts. They didn't look at me as I stumbled by with my shopping bags. They had their eyes closed, or else were looking at the ground. It made me uneasy. I was so close to them, and they were so foreign, so alien to me, and what they were doing was so obviously private. I wondered if their chant was a war-chant, or would put them in some state of mind in which they could not be held responsible for their actions. All the way across the field I kept looking back over my shoulder. From the far side I could just see the black tops of their heads still there, immobile as they lugubriously continued their solemnities. It struck me what a stoical, tedious thing native American ritual could be.

It was in that field that I met the snakes. There were green ones five feet long, and coal-black ones a yard long, and little grey ones with yellow livery stripes down their sides. Once I spotted one of the big green ones just as it heard me. It lay very still right across the path three feet ahead, its head and tail hidden in the long grass. It thought I couldn't see it. Very slowly I took a step backwards. Just as my cowboy heel came down it snapped around and darted towards me. I jumped back into the air and landed seven feet away. The snake then changed its mind and slithered away into the field. The next day I could still see the heel prints in the grass where I had landed, and tried to reproduce the spectacular backwards leap I had performed. I couldn't cover half the distance.

Another time I reached the ditch near the supermarket to find three of the grey snakes there before me, drinking from the puddle in the bottom. Slowly, reluctantly, they drew back into the brush to let me pass.

One overcast warm afternoon I reached the edge of the field on the way back and was suddenly overcome with fatigue. I decided to nap in the open air. I didn't want to risk sleeping with the snakes in the grass, though, and as I looked about for a safe bed I noticed a large willow tree nearby, with a big fork in the low branches. I hung my shopping bags from a bough and climbed into the tree.

The perch worked well, with my back against the trunk and my feet on the branches. I quickly fell into a deep sleep.

In the middle of it I had an odd dream. I dreamt that I felt the light turn orange on my eyelids and opened my eyes to see the sun peering out of the clouds. Ah, I thought, as if waking up: the sun is coming out. It was warm on my face. I smiled. Then I realized that I was not alone. I looked down. A man stood in the road below me, a local Indian dressed in leather and shells and feathers. He had a goatee beard and long grey hair. He grinned and pointed at me.

'Yes, yes,' he said. He laughed, and the sunlight accentuated the lines in his old face. He was delighted to see me up in the willow boughs. He pointed at me again, and said, 'Sunshine, tree.'

I laughed and nodded back. I thought he was pointing out that I had found a sunny spot in the tree. He seemed to be saying it as someone might sniff the seaside air and say: 'Ah! The sea.' Yes, he meant, it is good to be both in the sunshine and in the tree.

But then I wondered if he meant that I had found the 'Sunshine Tree', that this tree was in some way associated with sunshine.

He smiled and repeated the phrase. 'Sunshine Tree!'

Suddenly I realized that he meant something quite different. He was not talking about the tree, but about me. He was naming me. This was how the native Americans chose and bestowed names. It was the first time he had seen me, I was new to the territory, and the circumstances in which he had spotted me were in the sunshine, in the tree. So my name was Sunshine Tree.

When I woke up it was still a cloudy afternoon. A faint breeze rustled the plastic supermarket bags. I felt deeply refreshed, even though I had only slept for quarter of an hour. I looked down at the road: it was empty. But the dream seemed real, not like a dream at all. I was convinced a man had been there talking to me and that the sun really had come out. It was confusing. But as I walked home with my bags I felt I had been welcomed to Taos.

*   *   *

59

Taos kept reminding me of England. The trees, the skies, the dry summery meadows, the cloudy afternoons, all seemed familiar – even the air itself, which was soft and hazy, not bracing. When I walked through the long grass I remembered walking through fields around my mother's home when I was fourteen, going out with a canvas knapsack on my back and a guitar over my shoulder with my friend Sam, and with Robin Launcelot. Robin, the son of a Yorkshire vicar, was twice our age. He had a bushy brown beard, long hair parted in the middle, and was recovering from a psychotic turn induced by some bad opiates. My mother took him in. He needed a place to rest for a few months, and in her rambling, semi-inhabitable home she had plenty of spare rooms, most of them furnished with bare floorboards, peeling wallpaper and a camp bed. The whole house had the feel of an encampment. It was easy to accommodate extra people.

Sam, for example, spent most of the summer with us. He and I liked Robin, who spoke softly, mumbling into his beard, and would take half an hour to decide whether or not he wanted a cup of coffee. When you asked he'd say, 'Er, I don't know,' and then thirty minutes later he would turn to you with a radiant smile and say, 'Yes, yes, I will, thank you,' and you'd have to ask what he meant.

He sang his own songs to a dreamy strumming on the guitar. He often got the chords wrong but didn't notice, and we didn't mind. His songs were about love, and were full of mountains and valleys and spirits. He was a hippie casualty, but he taught me to play too, and the beaten-up red Spanish guitar I bought in a junk shop became my most treasured possession.

The anticipation of setting out to camp by the river with that guitar on my shoulder, knowing we would soon be building a fire and listening to Robin's songs and making tea with boiled river water and sleeping under the stars in sleeping bags and waking up all dewy in the sunshine – that feeling came back to me vividly now each time I stepped onto the plank across the ditch and entered the field leading to Smith's Supermarket.

Taos felt like the England of my childhood. It was partly the climate – being seven thousand feet above sea level, Taos is no warmer than an English town in summer, and clouds come over most days – and partly the hay fields and stands of willow and elm. But there was more. The very atmosphere – and not just that, but the spirit of the place – somehow echoed the English countryside of the 1970s. Maybe the liberal attitudes of the mid '70s lived on here still. Or maybe it was that the world I grew to know back then, in my early teens – the world of the Woodstock aftermath and Creedence Clearwater Revival, of Ten Years After, of late Beat poetry and Buddhism and the big, floppy guidebook to hippie life called *Be Here Now* – had been imported to England from just such towns as Taos. The '60s happened all over Europe and America, but Taos had been one of the epicentres. Or maybe it was just that I was changing, reverting to how I had been then, more awake, less distracted by worries. Maybe this was how any countryside could make you feel, and now I was starting to notice it again as I had done in my teens.

But there was something familiar, even ordinary about Taos, too. The town was far from ordinary, certainly: it had an old adobe plaza with an exotic bandstand. Out on the mesa old hippies lived in houses bunkered down into the earth and built out of old tyres and beer cans, then smothered in adobe. Odd devices protruded from their walls and roofs designed to generate electricity from light or wind. Kit Carson Street had the oldest boardwalk in America, and was lined with art galleries, and the town had thoroughly draped itself in its tourist guise, like an old Indian pulling on a poncho to shield himself from the cold. It had shielded itself with moccasin jackets hung on store fronts, with gallery windows full of lithographs of Indian maids and coyotes howling at the moon, with restored viga beams and retouched adobe walls, with old-fashioned western-style lettering above the store fronts, and with motels like the Sagebrush, a new adobe castle, and restaurants with neon cactus signs serving burritos and margaritas.

But behind all of that the real town, safely protected, went about its life with the ordinariness of any other little town – like the naked body beneath the clothes, that in private lies bare-limbed in an ordinary bathtub.

There was something comforting in this. I could understand why Taos attracted artists and writers. There wasn't much to do but get on with your work. You could go hiking in the mountains, you could ski in winter; you built fires at night because of the altitude. But even that – the bringing in of the logs, the rolling up of the newspaper, the stacking of the kindling – it all seemed straight-forward and plain, not exotic. It was like being at home.

Taos seemed a place where it would be easy to live the way you wanted. There was nothing to stop you. A man who drove an old brown Porsche with California plates used to visit our compound. Sometimes in the morning I would see his car there. Other times he came in the afternoon. Once I saw him stepping out of his car with a bunch of yellow roses. I never met him but I used to see him driving around town. He had a balding head and wore a brown leather jacket cut like a sports coat. I imagined he might be a scriptwriter up from Hollywood for the summer. He was free. He had the life of his choice. He worked on his writing some of the time and then drove over in a sports car to bring his girlfriend flowers. I never saw the woman he visited, who lived across from my unit, screened by a pine bush, nor did I ever exchange a word with him, but I liked him anyway.

Meanwhile I settled into a routine. I knew no one but didn't mind. I had taken myself on self-imposed retreats before, and this seemed to be another one. I enjoyed the chance to take attentive pleasure in small luxuries. Twice a week I allowed myself a burger at Ogilvie's Restaurant on the plaza, where the burgers were good and came with fries and a salad. After lunch I watched TV for twenty minutes. At tea-time I went for a walk, turning right on to the road out of our driveway. I strolled away from town, out of the trees, to where you had an unobstructed view of the mountains and could see the road heading off across the sage-covered plain. The tarmac was smooth and the twin yellow lines in the middle almost seemed luminous in the daylight. So little traffic used the road that often I walked along the lines, with visions of polished chrome tanker trucks and Mack cabs playing in my head. It was the summer of *Thelma and Louise*. This was a little piece of the big American road that they had embarked on. Once I even lay down on it and rested my forehead between the lines. This was as close as you could get to the road, I thought to myself. I thought about jumping in a car and going on a long trip, and decided this intimate taste of the road would do for now.

It dawned on me slowly that I was in the best possible place. Whether it was me or the town, Taos seemed to accept every foible, every laziness, every wasted hour, so that nothing seemed wasted. I had only to walk out my door and hear the breeze in the eucalyptus trees, or stroll along the road till I could see the bare mountains, or light a fire, lie on my back and listen to its crackling and watch the flickering on the ceiling, faint in the daylight, to find a peace I never knew in London. Just to be in Taos was an acknowledgement of a desire I had been suppressing for years. I had the sense that I was walking once again in a pair of boots I had not worn for many years, and which were the only boots that fitted me, that had been made for me and me alone. It was a relief to discover I could still experience such a sensation. I felt forgiven, for I didn't know quite what, as if I was ending years of self-exile.

I wondered about this. I thought back to a time at Cambridge when I had been acutely depressed. At the time I had been reading about spirit possession and shamanism in the anthropology museum, and in my debilitated state I was beginning to wonder whether I myself might have been possessed, by some dybbuk or demon. I remembered a moment of panic when I locked myself into a telephone cubicle tucked beneath the great stone staircase of the library and called a friend in London.

'You don't sound good,' she said when she heard my voice.

'I'm not,' I lamented. But when I tried to tell her what was wrong I found that the misery vanished. Instead of feeling relieved about this I felt scared. There seemed to be something malevolent inside me. It acted like a limpet when you touched it, attaching itself tightly to its rock so it couldn't be examined; or else disappearing like cockroaches in a kitchen at night as soon as you flick on the light – but the moment you close the door again and turn out the light, there the beetles are once more. It was the same with my unhappiness. As soon as I hung up the telephone, I knew it would be there again.

'What's wrong?' she asked.

I found I couldn't answer that. I was aware only of a mischievous grin hovering in my belly, as if a gargoyle had bundled the depression into a cupboard and now hung there guarding it. That was when I decided that I must be possessed. Finally I could almost see the dybbuk. It tortured me all day, then sat on the suffering and laughed when I attempted to address it.

'I'm just miserable,' I repeated, though it came out sounding blasé, everyday.

The pips started on the line. I rummaged in my pocket for another tenpence, shoving it in just in time.

She told me that once when she had been unhappy she had gone to a priest, and it had helped. I made up my mind then and there that I would get myself christened. I needed to have the seal inscribed on my forehead. The universe was too dangerous a place not to. Three weeks later I organized a christening service for myself, and four friends stood around the font holding candles and smiling in embarrassment.

I remembered that ceremony now. It got me thinking about the Flying Father again. It occurred to me that the reason I had been so impressed by him was perhaps that Christianity, up till now, had been my only bulwark against the deep fears that had emerged during that depression. He was an appealing kind of Christian, tough and outdoorsy, and ascetic, a latter-day equivalent of the old Celtic saints who rowed across the northern seas in coracles. I thought again about going over to his new town, Las Vegas, and trying to find him, and decided I would do it soon. In the end, though, a number of things were to get in the way of that trip.

But now I was aware of some other kind of security growing inside me. When I looked back over the last few years it seemed that I had been dragging myself through jobs and loves that meant little to me. I had settled into a life of permanent mild depression, not going away in search of what I lacked, yet never ceasing to believe that that was what I needed to do. I had neither committed myself to my life at home nor abandoned it, but had lived in a perpetual limbo. Later I went away now and then on assignments, yet oddly these didn't change things either. I became a clockwork toy. I would wind myself up with turns of despair and hope, then trundle off in one direction, wait there, winding myself up again in the same way, and move off once more. I stealthily set up my life to allow free rein to my mindless migratory urges. I travelled like a blind man who having once found his way to a bakery down certain streets continues time after time to walk to it even though the bakery has long since closed down. The croissants they sold him were so good that he refuses to give up the slender hope that *this* morning they will be there again, that he will smell the shop from the corner and soon be munching on the best breakfast he ever ate. Time after time he is disappointed, yet doesn't give up.

It was only now, in Taos, for reasons I could not explain, that things were finally and decisively changing. I felt like a teenager again, I remembered what life had been like before I began to worry about it. I was like a newly released prisoner who feels strange in his civilian shirt and realizes with a shock that he can walk all the way down the street if he chooses, and down the next one, and for a moment is dazzled by his freedom, by the sunlight and the open air, and doesn't know which way to go, what to do, there are so many pleasures.

Taos was full of pleasures. There were the hot springs in the gorge of the Rio Grande. I climbed down into the ravine on a dirt track, crossed a girder bridge, then stripped off and slipped into a hot, clear pool lined with green sand. When I got too hot I cooled off in the swift, brown river. I swam to a mud bank on the far side, where you could coat yourself in the black mud and watch it turn grey in the sunshine, feel it tighten on your skin, then swim back, washing it off, and once again turn pink in the hot pool.

There was the aroma of the piñon wood I burnt in my fireplace. And there was seeing the light fade outside my kitchen window while I chopped a carrot, an onion, a tomato for supper. There was driving out to the Rio Grande Gorge Bridge seven miles west of Taos, out on the mesa, in an old TransAm with a student called Basil, pronounced like *nasal*. The seven-hundred-foot gorge opened out so suddenly in the plateau that even from the carpark you couldn't see it. We drank two bottles of Dos Equis each on the way, and hurled them down from the middle of the span. They flew far out, then turned into flickering stars. We couldn't hear the smash when they landed. And there was the high hike up to Williams Lake in the mountains, the track leading up through alpine forests to a turfy, rock-strewn bowl among the peaks, with the poster-blue lake in the bottom. That was where the otters lived. On every rock scattered about the mossy ground otter families sat in the sunshine, chattering to one another, watching suddenly when we stood up and took a step. On the far side of the lake the sun glittered on a slope of scree shaken loose from the body of the mountain like a collapse of old flesh, acting as if separate from the grey bulk to which it belonged.

There was the pleasure of lighting my fire on a cold morning, pulling away the wrapper of the starter log which I allowed myself on chilly mornings to speed things up, and holding the match to the tears at either end, and going into the kitchen to make coffee knowing that the fire would be yellow and big when I came out and that the smell of the pine sap, a dark smell like incense, would already be drifting into the room, steeping the carpet, the curtain, my clothes, the bedcover, in its essence, and then at night falling asleep to the little plosive sounds and whisperings of the fire, feeling full to the brim with the sensations of the day.

Taos was full of pleasures.

SIX

A Point of Human Light

I GOT TO KNOW several people in Taos. The first was Lucia Trentinesi. I met her at the Taos pueblo, the ancient Indian settlement that has stood for hundreds of years outside town, an Escher-like cluster of apartment blocks built of dried mud.

The Indians were doing corn dances to Santa Ana that day. Ten men and women clad in white deer-leather were stomping around in a little square. They had feathers tied to their wrists and ankles, and necklaces of dyed corn kernels round their necks. Three men on plastic school chairs beat a lugubrious, unwavering beat on drums.

I watched for a while, thinking of D. H. Lawrence and the Indian dances he had seen in New Mexico, and the exhilarating insights he had had. All I experienced was boredom. It even looked as though the participants were bored. People said that these were not tourist dances, though tourists were allowed to watch, and it was easy to believe. I couldn't imagine any tourist staying for more than five minutes of the heavy, mindless stomping. There were in fact a handful of visitors in the pueblo that afternoon, but they milled about the village with cameras and Sony Handycam videos ignoring the dances. Whenever a new car pulled into the yard in the heart of the pueblo the new arrivals would hurriedly lock up, cross the wooden footbridge over the stream, and come panting up to the dancers. They would peer over shoulders, position themselves for shots of the costumes, then stand still, as if transfixed by the sudden deadening realization that they certainly needn't have rushed, that the dancers were going to plod on right through the afternoon. A few minutes later they would be gone, browsing the pottery and jewellery stores.

I liked being in the pueblo. One of the charms of a prosperous pueblo is that it has the feel of a city, even with only a thousand inhabitants. This is the feat of indigenous settlements the world over: the ability to make any small community a real centre of humanity, so that when you enter it you feel you have left the wastes behind. This is the sense the metropolitan sprawls fail to give. Their magnetism is a listless pull, some lode in the brain like the pigeons' compass guiding you there almost unwittingly.

Then it occurred to me that the boredom I felt before the dance might be a clue, a gateway to a mystery. After all, these dancers were clearly performing for neither their spectators' pleasure nor their own. So why were they doing it? They undertook it as an obligation. Their heavy, smooth faces drooped and sagged with the necessity, the tedium of it. For a moment my heart beat faster at the realization that it truly was a religious ceremony, that they were honouring something other-worldly, something bigger than themselves. They were doing it because there was something in the universe more important than their discomfort, their blistered feet, their weary limbs, and their boredom. They were beating into the earth with their feet their acknowledgement of the forces they didn't understand, that no one can understand, their rhythmic tribute to the existence of the corn seed and its germination. Here were people who had not forgotten the simple miracle of a field of corn. This dance was their clumsy, profound celebration.

But I had to keep reminding myself of that, and in the end I couldn't get it to work any more. My enthusiasm sank.

I walked about the pueblo for a while. It was four in the afternoon. It was good to be out walking on a cloudy afternoon in August with my sleeves rolled up and my cowboy boots dusty – after my encounters with the snakes in the field I had taken to wearing the boots whenever I went out – and nothing to do till six or seven, when I would make supper, build a fire, and read *The Count of Monte Cristo.*

I don't remember the first words I said to Lucia Trentinesi. We found ourselves walking down either side of the same track. Suddenly I was conscious of the silence between us. I spoke, she answered, laughing, in an Italian accent. We were immediately in a conversation.

By the time we reached her car, parked on the edge of pueblo land, I knew that she was studying native American literature for a Ph.D., that she came from a town near Milan, was staying in San Diego, California, for the summer, and had been in love with a Jew in Flagstaff, Arizona, for two years. Last summer she had flown out to visit him in his apartment and sat staring out the window at a July thunderstorm that fell upon the city while he told her he was leaving her for another woman. The other woman had been sitting in the coffee shop on the corner right then – she stressed this point – waiting for Lucia to leave, for her to hail a taxi and go back to the airport. The other woman, who was American, would be watching while she waited at the kerb for a cab.

'Can't I wait till the rain stops?' she asked him.

'I'll call a cab for you,' he said. 'It's fine. I have an account with them. I'll take care of it.'

That was when it hit her, she told me, when she heard that now he had an account with a taxi firm. That was new. He would never have opened an account before. It was a change. He was in a new life already. That was when she understood it was over.

I wondered why she told me all this within the first twenty minutes of meeting me. Was it because I was half Jewish, like him? Because she was in the south-west again, the theatre of her old love? Did I look like him? Was she crazy? Whatever it was, the opportunist in me decided it was auspicious. I took a chance. She had already offered me a lift back to town, and I suggested that, if she had time, instead of going straight back we should go up to

D. H. Lawrence's ranch first. It was twenty miles further north. I
pointed it out on the map.

She agreed without hesitation.

On the way she gave me more details of her last love. She had
met him by chance on a back street in Venice. It was incredible
how coincidental the important things in life were, she said. So
contingent, so accidental, yet they could be so big. They could
swallow up years of your life. I agreed. It was amazing what could
come of chance meetings, I said, aware now of an eager tension in
my abdomen.

By the time we turned off the road by the green sign saying,
'San Cristobal 5' onto a ribbed dirt track that shook the car, I
sensed it was inevitable. I didn't understand how it had happened.
Neither of us had cast a line, yet we were both hooked. She had
green-brown eyes, and whenever I glanced at her, our eyes met and
locked.

Later I met an astrologer who told me there was something special
about New Mexico that made it easy to get intimate with strangers.
There was something about the dry air, he said, and the altitude, and
the history of the place, its having been the epicentre of '60s free love,
that gave everyone the easy self-assurance of some mild intoxicant.
He himself had spent fifteen years riding New Mexico's easy current,
drifting from one intimacy to the next, guided, he told me, only by
the promptings of Eros. As soon as the visitation of the god was over,
he explained, you moved on too.

I now seemed to be entering a first-hand experience of this aspect
of New Mexico.

Lucia parked the car. A swathe had been cleared in the pine
trees and a little gravel track zigzagged up a few hundred feet to a
white mausoleum, the shrine that Frieda Lawrence had built for
her departed husband. We puffed up to it. In an urn topped by
a phoenix spreading its eagle wings, high above the altar, were
Lawrence's ashes. Frieda herself had been buried just outside the
door, beneath a slab.

We flipped through the visitors' book, then stood silently in the doorway gazing over the huge green plain that stretched away in front of us. We were high above it on the even slope of the mountain, and the mesa stretched all the way to Arizona. We could see the dark-blue smoke cloud of mountains on the state line, one hundred and fifty miles away. And all around the pine trees were hissing in the wind, making the only sounds. Occasionally one of them groaned, a sharp, wild, animal-like croak.

We walked down two bends of the zigzagging path and sat on a bench. There was a curious urgency in the hissing of the trees, as if the sound was about to break into some other greater noise, and in the presence of the odd little mausoleum up above, behind us, like some Catholic reliquary from an Italian graveyard perched there on the wild mountainside, and in the knowledge that this was the view Lawrence had seen, and this the place that he claimed had affected him more than any other. 'Nowhere else ever changed me from the outside,' he said of his ranch at Taos.

I was puzzled. I remembered reading that from his ranch he could see the lights of Ranchos de Taos at night. Ranchos, a small district of Taos, lay thirty miles south of here, just on the far side of the town, hidden not only by innumerable trees but also by at least one great shoulder of mountain. And realizing that he had plucked the name out of his memory, while writing about New Mexico at a table in Naples, gave me a rush of excitement. It didn't matter. Accuracy, correctness – these things were unimportant. They were the chaff of life. Real life was the inspiration in you. Life was like Sappho's love: 'Love shakes me as the wind shakes the oak leaves on the hillside.' That was exactly what love did, and what life could do. Lawrence's great gift to the world, and especially to England, was precisely that blast of raw energy, raw love, unedited life. That was all that mattered. The little intricacies, the devices and tie-ups in a life, could take care of themselves. The important thing was to make room always for the big powers of life, to be wide-open inside, spacious and strong.

72

Meanwhile, things were leaping ahead with Lucia. I had heard stories of random couplings between strangers before, but always doubted them. One friend of mine claimed to have knocked on a door at an Oxford college to borrow a pen, and to have emerged an hour later, sated and exhilarated. Another friend had a similar story about a train journey. Then there were all the aeroplane stories. I could hardly believe it, but now it seemed to be happening to me.

Lucia had been gradually sliding her slight body closer and closer to mine. Now she was leaning against me in fake fatigue. It all happened fast. Afterwards I could barely reconstruct how it came about. All I could remember was her long, straight, black hair, her heavy eyebrows, her smooth tapered Italian cheeks and lips. When she touched my elbow I sensed how light her arm was, and I remembered her crossing her legs and her denim mini-skirt riding an inch higher. I also remembered her telling me she was like a lake, and not believing she could possibly mean what she seemed to mean.

I put my arm round her shoulder. She snuggled into my chest, and I felt the movement deep in my belly. I knew what she wanted to do. I moved my arm and before I even began to steer her she turned to face me, then stood up and straddled my lap. Before I knew what was happening her tongue was in my mouth.

I felt like bursting out laughing. I put all my energy into fighting the smile that threatened to break into my face. I was sure she would pull back if she felt it. I tried to work out what I had done to make this happen, but couldn't make sense of it and gave up. I decided it wasn't me, it wasn't her, it wasn't Lawrence's shrine. It was this place, this hissing forest and the yawning view cut out of the forest before us. It demanded a response, an action.

A minute later she said the thing about being like a lake and to my amazement stood up and removed her panties, bypassing all the more superfluous stages. We had met less than an hour before.

Afterwards we lay back at either end of the bench with our legs intertwined. I finally let my laughter go. I was still caught in a gale of testosterone intoxication, and the laughter came billowing up from some dark place in the depths of my belly, as if from a healed but still tender wound. Marvin Gaye singing 'Sexual Healing' ran through my mind, and then a huge tenderness for D. H. Lawrence welled up. He seemed so unforgiving, so dictatorial, so Nietzschean. His was a demanding aesthetic of life. Yet now it seemed that what I had really gleaned from my adolescent reading of his work was tenderness. The only message I could hear now in his writing was one of an endlessly forgiving love. He didn't demand obeisance to the nether forces, as people said, as even he said. Rather, he understood and forgave the human urge for coupling, for love. He encouraged it and in doing that he supported humanity to the bottom of its being. I wondered now how I could ever have been scared of him.

A hawk swerved across the sky, then dived into the trees, twitching its bent-back wings to hold the course true in the wind. The dark, crude-oil laughter came bubbling out of me again, and I realized with a sudden grateful relief why I had come to New Mexico. I had come for love. I had come to find out how to love, how to be loved, how to love myself. Until I learned that, I had no chance of discovering who I really was. I felt as if a house was falling down all around me, but instead of being afraid I stood watching it collapse with only curiosity and relief. My life had been a long struggle to hide from myself, and now all my walls of concealment were coming down. How and why were unimportant. It was happening, and all I could do was laugh. My belly felt like a great dark cave, huge. I had never before realized how big I was inside, how much space there was in me for love.

The tumult of joy began to subside. For a moment I was afraid that after this revelation I could only suffer depression. But then I felt the woman at the other end of the bench slowly stretch out her right leg, bringing the foot to rest on my chest, and I relaxed again, smiled. It didn't matter if the vision faded. I was caught in the thick of life whether I wanted it or not. The joy was not an event within my head, but an endless event all around me, in which I had no choice but to participate. And right then I could and would share the ecstasy with this new woman. I didn't need to utter a word about it. All I needed to do was show her, live it with her, inscribe it all over her with my actions. Words, now, seemed like chaff in the wind. The big cavern of consciousness inside me needed to speak not in words but in deeds, in motions, in embraces.

We strolled down the gravel switchbacks to the ranch house, a small wooden cabin with a painting of a pastel-blue buffalo on the side. It resembled the beasts of the Lascaux cave paintings, and Lawrence had apparently done it himself.

I learnt this from the caretaker at the ranch, who lived in the big house next to the cabin. He looked in his seventies, wore a cap and had a small elf-like face. He limped out of the door with a stick as soon as we reached the yard in front of his office, as if he had been waiting for us. He mumbled, 'Welcome to the San Cristobal Ranch where D. H. Lawrence stayed on three separate occasions over a three-year period,' and briefly shook my hand, then took both of Lucia's hands and held them for a long time. The thought crossed my mind that perhaps he had been able to see us up on the bench. It looked as though trees stood in the way, and the fence of the yard. I tried to gauge the view he had from the office window. It was hard to tell.

'Come and see the cabin where the Lawrences lived and ate and cooked and did everything else they did,' he said in one big breath, eyeing us nervously to see if his speech had impressed us.

He pulled Lucia off out of his little yard. I followed.

The cabin was a simple two-room house with uneven floors and low ceilings. On the table stood an ancient typewriter. The caretaker stressed that it was not Lawrence's typewriter but authentically one from the period. I knew anyway that Lawrence wrote in notebooks. I remembered a passage from his Italian travels when he sits himself down among the roots of a great oak tree and writes there in its shade while surveying the Tuscan hills.

There was a big fireplace, its rear wall stained black, and a bare double mattress resting on a wooden bedframe. The caretaker limped over to the chimney and leaned under the mantel. 'Come here,' he called us. We walked over. He took Lucia's hand and pulled her towards him. She hesitated. 'Look up there,' he said, moving his hand to her hip in a pretence of helping her lean under. She backed away, alarmed.

'Come on, come on,' he barked. 'Come and look.'

She pretended not to understand.

'I'll look,' I offered. I stooped under. It was a wide chimney and it reached straight up to a big square of light sky.

'It's big,' I said, assuming that it was the size of it that he wanted to show off, though in fact it wasn't as big as the chimney in the house in which I grew up. But when I ducked out again he wasn't there anymore. Both he and Lucia had gone outside. For an instant I felt like the husband in the famous Boccaccio story: while he is busy inspecting the inside of the clay jar, his wife is busy cuckolding him with the man selling it.

There was a small lawn outside. The caretaker was standing beneath a great pine tree holding Lucia's hand and trying to persuade her to lie down on a bench. She was cautious about doing it. I was convinced by now that he must have spied on us. Whether or not he actually hoped to induce her, or even us, to perform again, he was certainly seized by a fit of prurience. Unless he was always this way. It seemed possible that he might regard himself, being the guardian of D. H. Lawrence's ranch, as the inheritor of Lawrence's mantle of sexual authority. For one deflating moment he even seemed an appropriate warden of Lawrence's history: a small wiry lascivious man who thought he was being clever and knowledgeable when he was being verbose. Somehow it seemed inevitable that after his death Lawrence should fall into the hands of people who reflected the worst sides of his nature.

I said, 'We better go. It's getting late.'

'No, no, no,' the guard replied. 'Just lie back and look up. This is the Georgia O'Keeffe Tree.' He was referring to Georgia O'Keeffe's famous picture of the branches and trunk of a tree viewed vertically from beneath. The painter had apparently lain back on this very bench to get the perspective.

Reluctantly Lucia tried it, and quickly stood up.

'There,' he said triumphantly. 'You see? Not so bad, not so bad.' He spoke to her in loud simple statements now, since she had pretended not to understand him.

I tried it. You could see the trunk tapering off into the sky and the swirling network of boughs that O'Keeffe had captured on her canvas.

Meanwhile he had walked over to the fence of the little garden and began to howl into the trees. I wondered what new trick he had up his sleeve when two pale fox-like dogs came trotting up to the fence.

'Sing!' he howled at them. 'Sing!'

They stiffened their tails and began to bark in clear, soprano yelps. Then sure enough they started to sing, letting out a crescendo of high falling cries that gradually prolonged themselves into musical howls. They were pet coyotes.

'Can we go in?' I asked.

'You try and touch them they'll take off your hand,' he told me with a grin.

We couldn't get away before we had signed the visitors' book in his office and written our addresses and listened to the details of his plans for a forthcoming trip to Italy. Several times he mentioned that he would like to include Milan in his itinerary. Lucia refused to take the hint.

As we drove away I wondered why we hadn't left sooner. But there was a curious allure to the place, a magnetism, and even he, with his hustling lasciviousness, had seemed to belong there. Besides, we both felt embarrassed by what we had done, and by our as yet unshared guess that we had been spied on.

It was getting dark when we reached Taos, and we went straight to the supermarket. I felt relieved when I finally opened the door into my studio with two brown paper bags of groceries in my arms.

Lucia called the hotel where she was staying, which was down in Albuquerque, and told them she wouldn't be back till the next day. She was flying back to San Diego the following afternoon. Meanwhile I found myself trembling again on this new drug, now that we were alone once more. She was too. She tripped over the corner of the coffee table and laughed nervously when I caught her, and her hands shook as she pulled sheets of newspaper out of the *Taos News* and rolled them up to make a fire. Night was falling outside. The windows had turned mauve. It reminded me of the end of day during term-time when I was a child, with the weather cold and rainy outside, the house cosy and yellow within. It was maritime weather, weather that made you want to drink whisky and sit in a little dock-side pub and wrap up in a donkey jacket.

I went into the bathroom. She had rinsed her underclothes and hung them from the shower rail. They were translucent now, the colour of an English sky. I walked back into the room to find the fire flickering and crackling, and it suddenly struck me that I felt more at home right then than I ever had in my life. Every step I took, every word I said, everything I did only made me feel more at home. I threw the cover from the bed onto the floor in front of the fire, and welcomed her into my new home.

SEVEN

The Lawrence Oils

THE NEXT PERSON I got to know was the owner of the La
Fonda Hotel on the plaza. It was a bizarre hotel, an adobe castle
with a cavernous lobby in which hung disturbing portraits of
troubled faces, and framed newspaper clippings from around the
world mentioning the hotel. The foyer was quite out of proportion
to the rest of the hotel, which consisted of tiny rooms furnished
with hand-painted dressers. But the hotel was an historic site: not
only did famous painters and writers of the 1930s stay in it, in
Taos's heyday, but it also housed the largest collection anywhere
of D. H. Lawrence's oil paintings.

The ten 'Lawrence Oils' were kept in the study of the man who
owned it. He was even more bizarre than his hotel. A Greek by
the name of Teddy Sakarios, he had moved to Taos in the '50s,
and lived alone in one of the small hotel rooms, his bed surrounded
by towers of books and boxes of memorabilia. His daily routine
had him out of bed in time to lunch in one of the town's finer
restaurants, with some local or visiting dignitary – an actress, an
assistant district attorney, a Colorado mayor – after which he
returned to the hotel for coffee at around four or five, where he
changed into his silk dressing gown and pottered about in his study,
which he had been tidying up and organizing for the past five years.
You could see why it had taken so long. The room, like his bedroom, was piled high with magazines and books. Clippings lay
everywhere, as if a fan had been aimed at a great pile of papers
on the desk. Clad in his silks, rabbit-like with his bushy white

moustache and sideburns, he would sit contentedly amid the mess till five each morning, shifting papers about, searching for old letters he once enjoyed, then settling down behind his desk to read them.

When I went into the dark hotel it was four o'clock in the afternoon. The receptionist, an ageing westerner in a denim shirt and white vest, asked how long I'd be staying, and told me the rates.

'I just want to see the paintings,' I said.

'Very good. That'll be a dollar, sir.'

I was lucky. Just after I handed over my dollar bill the owner himself came slowly down the entrance hall, his shadow lengthening over the gleam of the tiles. He stopped beside me, rotund, beaming, looking like a man who has just enjoyed a good dinner, and nodded slowly. 'Welcome!' he said.

'Thank you.'

He kept on nodding. 'Wait a moment,' he said. He called to the assistant to give me some cards and disappeared through a doorway hidden in the panelling. The receptionist placed four postcards on the counter, all showing the same view of the hotel lobby.

When Teddy came back he had removed the black velvet jacket he had been wearing and replaced it with a purple silk robe. He smiled at me again and invited me to follow. He spoke so softly that I could barely hear him, and he moved very softly too – I noticed that he was wearing only white socks on his feet – leading me into a small room lined with filing cabinets. Paintings and photographs and pictures cut out of magazines covered the walls. There were several signed photographs of nude women reclining on rocks in seductive poses.

'Girlfriends?' I asked.

He chuckled, then cleared his throat.

'This, this, this.' He went around pointing out the Lawrence paintings. When he had designated all ten pictures he turned to me and said: 'How much?'

I frowned.

'How much you think? Just think?'

'You mean how much are they worth?'

He grinned.

'I've no idea.'

He reached down behind his desk, opened a drawer and handed me a letter. It was apparently from an LA art dealer who had found a museum interested in acquiring the Lawrence Oils. He said that a figure in excess of five million dollars did not strike him as unrealistic. On the contrary, he thought he might raise twice as much.

'Look,' Teddy told me, gesturing at the paintings with a big smile. 'Then tell me what you think.'

The way he was looking at me made me think he had some trick up his sleeve, some trump card he was about to play – but apparently it was just his natural manner, for after I had spent a little while inspecting the leering faces, muddied colours, and dismal landscapes of the paintings, he had no further startling information to give me. At least not right away.

I said I had no idea but perhaps the dealer was right.

He flicked up his eyebrows in a merry, knowing way. He had bought the paintings from Frieda, Lawrence's widow, for next to nothing, and was now confidently a paper-millionaire.

Most of them were painted in Italy, and Lawrence accordingly signed them 'Lorenzo'. Years ago I had read Lawrence's advice on how to paint well. The important thing, he said, was to enter fully into the picture, into the oils and the brushes, to be completely absorbed by them at the time of execution. I had been impressed by this advice, though I never acted on it. Now, looking at Lawrence's work, I found myself doubting its wisdom.

The pictures reached the Taos Fonda via a circuitous route: first to the Albemarle Gallery in London, where in 1919 Lawrence's exhibition was closed down immediately after its opening on grounds of obscenity. On the first day a policeman entered the gallery and turned the canvases to the wall. It was the happiest fate the paintings could have known: instant notoriety yet the very minimum of scrutiny. Not only are they dull paintings, they are

81

also hardly obscene. The leering faces may have fat, ugly lips, but the nudity is less explicit than even Botticelli's. Lawrence could not have been luckier. Except that a court order followed demanding immediate destruction of the works. Lawrence succeeded in obtaining a stay of execution provided the paintings left British shores at once, never to touch them again. So they were shipped to New Mexico, where, some twenty years after Lawrence's death, Frieda passed them on to her close friend Teddy.

I knew the outlines of the story already, but there were a few more things I was to learn about Lawrence's fate from Mr Sakarios.

'Look!' Teddy was pointing at a framed letter on the wall. It was a letter from the La Fonda de Taos Inn addressed to Margaret Thatcher. It was from him, dated 1984. In it he offered to give the Lawrence Oils back to the British people. The only catch was that he wanted the British people to give the Elgin Marbles back to Greece in exchange. There was no reply. Beside the letter hung a second one, similar but addressed to Neil Kinnock, prefaced by Teddy's best wishes for success in the forthcoming general election. It suggested that in his pending premiership the next leader might consider the same offer. There was a reply from a private secretary: 'Mr Kinnock does not believe that the *quid pro quo* basis you suggest of the Elgin Marbles for the Lawrence Oils would be acceptable.' In the event, of course, Mr Kinnock's opinion was to prove irrelevant.

I browsed around the study. The plate glass covering the desk held down many little scraps torn from papers and books and magazines – poems, letters, amusing anecdotes. One joke from a newspaper that he had inserted under the glass must have been there to remind him of his native land: 'Heaven is where the cooks are French, the police British, the mechanics German, the lovers Greek, and everything is organized by the Swiss; Hell is where the cooks are British, the police German, the mechanics French, the lovers Swiss, and everything is organized by the Greeks.'

He showed me some love letters from a French actress famous in the 1960s, whom I had never heard of, and opened up an old magazine to a nude spread she had done. The colours had faded to the '50s hues of Ladybird books, and the exuberantly absurd poses had dated sadly. They weren't remotely alluring.

Sensing that my interest was not as piqued as it might have been, Teddy then played the trump card that he had in fact been holding back ever since he discovered that I was British, a fellow country-man of Lawrence's.

'You know what happened to Lawrence after he died?' he asked.

I did know. They had buried him in the graveyard at St Paul de Vence in the Riviera, where he had been staying in a sanatorium. A few weeks later Frieda disinterred his body, cremated it, and flew the ashes out to New Mexico, where she erected the shrine at the ranch with the phoenix on top.

'That's what you think,' Teddy said, his grin spreading. 'You want to know what really happened?'

'Sure.'

'OK. But first.' He stepped over a box to reach a filing cabinet, from which he extracted a bottle of ouzo and two tequila glasses. Very slowly, his hand trembling, he poured out two shots on the desk and handed me one with wet fingers. The glass was wet too but he didn't seem to notice. He raised his glass and nodded at me. 'To Lawrence. He has been good to us all.'

We drank.

'After he died,' he began, his voice a little stronger now – though he still spoke slowly, stalling and grinning as if he knew something I would very much like to know – 'they didn't bury him.'

He stared at me, his green eyes shining and his cheeks bright. He seemed to expect some response.

'What?' I said.

'No.' He shook his head. 'They didn't bury him. Frieda, Lady Brett and Mabel Dodge Luhan.' He raised a hand and counted off three fingers as he enumerated the final entourage. 'You know what they did?'

'What?'

He opened his mouth, bared his teeth, and chomped. Without a word he nodded again, grinning.

'No.'

He kept on nodding slowly. 'They did.'

'No.'

'Why not? They want his power. So they do it. Yes. All three of them. They eat him.'

He poured out another shot of ouzo for each of us. 'Here. Drink. To Frieda, a dear friend.'

We knocked them back. He set down his glass with a little clink on the desk, then raised a forefinger to his lips. He stared at me, holding the finger there.

I nodded.

He beckoned me past his desk. 'This is my mother.' He pointed to a woman in black wearing an elaborate black headdress. She was standing among a group of Indian dignitaries in the middle of the Taos pueblo. She was the spitting image of Madame Bouboula in the film *Zorba the Greek*. Beside her, clad in a feather headdress that had apparently been offered him as an honour, stood Teddy himself.

'Three years she lived with me here, but now she's dead and I have girlfriends. Girlfriends everywhere, all over the world.'

He opened up more drawers to show me handfuls of letters from his girlfriends all over the world. It struck me then what a lonely man he was, living in his small world, buttressed by the paraphernalia of a glamorous past that had faded. No longer did Lawrence and Huxley and O'Keeffe come for cocktails in the Fonda Hotel. Taos still had its writers, but it had lost its glamour. It was a tourist town, and a serious, quiet, small town too, but it was no longer a resort for the international intelligentsia.

Teddy offered me another ouzo, but the first two had gone to my head. It was already six o'clock and I felt if I didn't leave soon I'd be there all night.

I thanked the lonely hotelier. He offered me another pile of the hotel postcards. I patted my breast and repeated my thanks.

'Come back,' he said. 'I tell you things make your hair stand up.' He tugged a handful of his white locks into the air to illustrate his point, revealing a large bald circle, and opened his eyes wide. 'Taos is a strange place,' he said.

EIGHT

The Monster

I HAD BEEN THINKING about making my way over to Las Vegas the following day, catching a bus there and back, to see if I could find the Flying Father, but something came up. While having a drink in the Old Taos Inn that evening, I met the movie producer. I found myself sitting at the next table to his in the foyer of the hotel, sipping a Dos Equis beer, watching the couples come and go. It was a good place to sit alone, a high room, more or less round, built out of old adobe and big viga beams, with a single giant tree trunk standing in the middle, rising up some forty feet like a tent post in a circus. It had been shaved down into small, even faces, and painted with a clear varnish, and it lent the presence of a totem pole to the room, made it feel like a good place to gather.

The movie producer and I got talking. I saw him drain a margarita and make his way through a second, and by the time our conversation sprang up he was in good spirits. He wore a peculiar outfit, and it was that which initiated our talk. A short waistcoat that reached only just below the armpits, covered in multi-sectioned pockets, white pads, pieces of grey wool and many buckles, then a pair of slacks, an army shirt, a pair of large outdoor boots, and John Lennon sunglasses. It looked like he must have been up to something, dressed for a specific activity, if not for a movie set, and it was only a matter of time before I asked him what he was doing in Taos.

'Passing through,' came the obscure reply. 'Just passing through.'

There was a touch of Jack Nicholson, I decided, in his relaxed pose, one ankle spaciously hooked up on the opposite knee, and in his speech, which was broad and quite loud.

I nodded.

A silence ensued. I wasn't sure how to follow up on my opening.

'How about yourself?' he came back, after finishing off his drink with a satisfied sigh.

'Me too,' I said. Then wondered if that was right. 'I've been here two weeks,' I added.

'Uh-huh. Two weeks.' He paused, turned his glass round. 'Well, I got in just an hour ago and I'll be on the road first thing.'

I asked where he was going, in the hope it might explain his garb.

'San Juan,' he replied.

'What are you doing up there?'

'Only one thing to do in San Juan. I guess you're not from these parts?'

I shook my head.

'Well, San Juan is famous all over the west, all over the country, practically, for one thing.'

He stopped, so I asked the question he was evidently waiting for: 'What would that be?'

'Fish. Trout. Biggest wild trout in America. Water comes off the dam into the San Juan river, perfect conditions, and you get monsters. Twenty-, twenty-two-inch rainbows, thirty-inch browns. I pulled a ten-pound rainbow out of that river last year. And I put it back. It'll be even bigger by now. Didn't have the heart to finish it off. Fish that size, you gotta respect it. As a matter of fact, I'm kind of hoping to run into it again. See how it's doing. Yeah, that's what I'm doing up in San Juan – I got an appointment with a fish.' He laughed hoarsely.

I said, 'We don't have trout that size in England.'

'That right?'

He waved to the barman and ordered us both another drink.

'You're on the Mexican brew,' he commented.

'Good stuff,' I said, feeling a little overawed by him.

'Can't beat the Chihuahua firewater, though. No, sir. Sure you won't join me in one? Make the best damn margaritas outside of LA here.'

I laughed. 'You can get a good margarita in LA?'

'Sure you can. You can get good anything in LA.'

The drinks arrived, the waiter setting out two white napkins on the producer's table, then placing the cocktail and the beer on them.

'And bring us some of that salsa of yours. That hot stuff.' He turned to me. 'Come on over here.'

I left my table and settled in opposite him.

'So anyway,' he said, as if about to return to a subject, but promptly forgetting what the subject was. 'So anyway,' he repeated, then had a pull on his drink.

Then he remembered. 'You ever been fishing?'

'Sure.' I related my adventures on the east coast working for a trawlerman and a trap-fisherman.

'How about real fishing? Fly fishing?'

'Couple of times. Caught a twelve-inch rainbow once.'

He nodded seriously. 'Nothing like it, right? Being out there in the water, just you and that fish and how are you gonna outsmart him. San Juan is the most technical river in America.'

I assumed this meant it was difficult to fish. 'You wear waders?'

'Neoprene suit. Stand in water up to here.' He indicated a line half-way up his chest.

My curiosity about his dress was answered, but I found myself curious about him now. He had a certain verve, a certain boisterous zest, that was appealing. He came from LA, apparently, and it seemed plausible he might be some film star I didn't know, or didn't recognize. I asked him what he did.

'Only two things to do in LA, act and produce, and I produce.'

'Produce movies?'

'Sure.'

I asked if I might have seen any of his films.

He listed off four, all of which I had seen, and which had been big box-office hits. I nodded. I wasn't sure how to react. He must have known it was an impressive list, but presumably a man of his stature was used to being known in advance, and in some confusion, I mumbled, 'Great movies.'

'Thank you,' he said, looking down. 'Glad you liked 'em.'

It was odd. He had this manner about him that suggested some elder statesman of Hollywood, something like a lightweight John Huston or even Orson Welles, yet he couldn't have been over forty-five. He had short, neat black hair just greying at the temples, and long, thin sideburns and a blue unshaven face. It occurred to me that he might be at the tail end of a binge. Perhaps he had come out to New Mexico on a sudden drunken whim. That was the kind of thing Hollywood people did, I thought. But if so, it seemed odd that he had come alone, although it was conceivably a faintly mawkish drunken move to want to go off fishing by oneself all of a sudden.

'You always fish alone?' I asked.

'Nah,' he replied, almost sneering. He was silent a moment, then he inhaled slowly as if coming to a momentous decision, drawing himself up, and announced: 'Fact is, I flew out from LA with my lady but when we got to Albuquerque she got on the first plane back down. Said I made some dumb promise or something about not having a snifter on the plane.' He chuckled. 'That's what you chaps call it, no? A snifter. So I said, the heck with it, you think you're going to spoil my fishing? I'll go up on my own, damn it.' His accent coarsened as he went on, until he stopped himself short suddenly and forced out an unconvincing laugh, then fell silent. He frowned, looking remorseful. He shook his head.

Trips could often put a strain on things, I offered. It wasn't much solace, nothing like what the empty glass had promised before it was empty.

'Yeah, well.' He waved at the barman. 'So anyway, here I am.

You ever gone fishing?' he asked, brightening up at the thought, as if it were a new one.

'Yes,' I repeated, and once again told him my brief anthology of fishing experiences.

'Well, I tell you what. I've got two sets of gear in the car. No sense having it rot there. You get your fanny down here at five o'clock sharp tomorrow morning and you've got yourself a fishing trip.'

He rotated his finger at the barman, indicating a repeat of the round, unaware that my new beer was still full, and said, 'Deal? What do you say?' He held out his hand.

Before I could give the matter any thought, I said, 'Deal,' and shook, still reeling from the shock of that word 'fanny': it had taken me a moment to remember what it meant in America.

After I left, I felt a little uneasy about what I had let myself in for. He was evidently drunk, and who knew what he would be like when he was sober in the morning. I hadn't even checked how long the fishing trip was supposed to be. He had mentioned a day's fishing, but did that mean I would be back in Taos tomorrow night? And although I had once caught a trout I had also spent a number of hours attempting to disentangle lines and hooks from chains of Gordian knots that my casting technique had created. I wasn't sure he would take kindly to having his gear mishandled. On the other hand, the idea of participating in the tail end of a little piece of Hollywood extravagance was inviting. I decided that a man with such successes behind him, and presumably with the kind of network of grand friends he must have, would scarcely have any motive for duplicity of any kind, or even for being unpleasant. After all, he was trusting me, whom he barely knew, so why shouldn't I trust him? Surely one of the best sides of success in the movies was to be able to bestow largesse wherever one wished: excessively, conspicuously, extravagantly.

Back in the studio I set my alarm clock for four-thirty.

*   *   *

After an hour and a half on the road we stopped for breakfast at a simple, linoleum-floored place called the Moosehead Diner. It was still dark when we went in, and cold, for we had climbed up through birch and pine forests into the mountains north-west of Taos. We ate a stack of pancakes each, silently guzzling cups of coffee. After breakfast the movie producer ordered four glasses of water and a giant coke, for the road, a drink he kept jammed between his legs on the velvet seat of the rental car. The sky began to turn glassy and clear, and soon you could make out the silent, soft desert reaching away to either side, a pale suede colour against the pellucid pre-dawn sky. He tuned in to a Country and Western station on the radio as we sped along, till finally we reached the edge of a deep, sandy canyon. At the bottom was a grey river.

He turned off the radio.

'Well, there she is. The San Juan.'

To the right was a great curving dam, and a green lake beyond it. From the foot of the dam flowed the river, fast and cold-looking, and ominously industrial at that early hour, a copper-green run-off from the great sheet of concrete. It was light now, but the sun was hidden behind low mountains, which had formed a mauve sil- houette edged with a filament of white-hot wire. Above them the sky was white where the sun would soon rise, while the canyon below us was filled with a soft blue light. It was like looking down into a vast cathedral.

We wound down into it and parked at the roadside. The pro- ducer opened up the trunk and began kitting himself out. He grunted quietly as he pulled off his trousers, donned a pair of thick thigh-length socks, then stepped into his neoprene suit. It was a sleeveless suit, like a pair of dungarees. Once he had it comfortably on he put his big boots on again, lacing them tightly, then tied a belt high up around his waist and pulled on his waistcoat. He opened up a plastic case and began sticking fly-hooks to the various pieces of foam and fur and wool on his vest, which were there for their ability to snag a hook securely but release it to a firm tug.

Also attached to the waistcoat were a little pair of fishing-line clippers, which looked like portable nail-clippers, a wooden landing net like an old tennis racket, on the end of a lightweight chain that wound itself up automatically inside a small chrome case, and a number of spools of line hanging from a set of clips. When fully freighted, with a deerstalker cap and a pair of pilot's Ray-bans, he looked the complete one-man band.

He then set about preparing two rods: fitting the sections together, clipping on the reels, tying on the leaders, knotting the hooks, biting on lead shot. Throughout all of these operations he said nothing. His hands shook, so it took several attempts to get each of the little knots tied, and he groaned periodically and mumbled to himself, but I was impressed that with the kind of hangover he must have been carrying he was able to do anything at all. When the rods were ready he laid them side by side on the roof of the car, then went to fetch something from the glove-box. I couldn't see what it was, but in the quiet of that early hour, the only sound being the faint rush of the river below, I heard the click of a cap, the glug-glug of a flask, a sharp sigh. He came back zipping up a pocket of his waistcoat, and said, 'All *right*!' as if now we could really get down to business, and started fitting me out with the spare gear.

We trooped off into the tall grass, bearing our rods like spears. There were a hundred yards to cross before we reached the river, and the rushes quickly rose up high over our heads. It was stiff and dry and it took some effort to push a way through. After some time we came to the bank of a small creek, a backwater off the main channel. It was only some fifteen feet wide, but it looked deep. I wondered what we would do to get across. I expected the producer to turn one way or the other along the bank, but to my surprise he marched straight on in. I waited. He marched right across, the water rising up to his chest at the deepest. I hesitated a moment, then followed him. It was strange to feel the cool pressure of the morning water gradually rise up my legs, around my loins, over my belly, and yet not get wet. I stepped up the opposite bank dripping, followed the producer's wet trail, already looking forward to the next crossing. It made you feel powerful to walk through water like that, without getting wet.

From close up the river looked quite different: a rich, translucent rusty brown. Big smooth pebbles lay on the bottom. Here and there you could make out strands of weed trailing in the current like scarves opening out in a breeze, and sometimes a swift stealthy shape shifted position in the stream. You could see at once that the river was rich with fish. It was deep, fast, cool and clean: a perfect trout river.

The producer spent a long time staring at the water, then stepped down into it and we began a long, heavy walk upstream. After only a few paces my thighs began to ache against the current, and I was amazed that he managed to keep going for so long. When we finally stopped, some two or three hundred yards up, on the outside of a wide bend, his face was shiny with sweat.

'OK,' he said, breathing heavily. 'You try this channel right here for a while, and I'll cross over and try the other side. We can switch over in half an hour or so. Sound good?'

I planted my feet on the bottom, and began my casts. I used a short line, trying to get it to lay itself out gently on the surface so as not to scare the fish, then drift down past me in a lazy coil. As soon as it started to straighten out again, swinging slowly in towards me, I pulled it in and flicked it upstream once more. I knew the fish were there: every time I shifted my boots on the bottom, kicking up a cloud of silt from among the pebbles, I would see two or three grey shadows disappear into the fertile murkiness I had created.

The only sound was the gurgle of the river, which sometimes acquired a deep reverberation. It was cool but pleasant standing up to my chest in the water. Above I could see the line of shadow retreating down the wall of the canyon, the lucid darkness draining out like an unwanted lymph, leaving the world pure, fresh, new.

It was a perfect time to be out in the river with a rod. The repeated flicking of the line, and the wait while it drifted down, and the flick once again, soon lulled me like a meditation, and I found myself relaxing into a mood of tranquil contemplation. Once I glanced over at the producer. He was standing in mid current busily tying some new fly on his line. I resumed my casting, feeling pleased that I had run into this man. I had never been trout-fishing in America before.

It was when my mood was at its dreamiest, while I was reflecting on the magnificence of this desert canyon with its powerful river, that it happened. I had more or less forgotten that the powerful river was full of powerful fish. There was no sudden tug, no leaping out of the water, and I didn't strike. There was just a trembling, living presence on the line all of a sudden. I remembered to tip up my rod and stood there dumbly watching as the reel whirred and the line went out. I had no idea what kind of a fish it was – a baby or a monster – but I knew that whatever it was I would give it all the time it needed before I tried anything.

The line veered off across the river. Then it went quite fast downstream, then even faster back upstream, a long way in a diagonal towards the opposite bank fifty yards upriver. It seemed to stay there for a while. The reel slowed down to a light clicking, then went quiet. I began to reel in the slack. Then suddenly I had reached the end of it, and it felt like I had touched a live object with my bare fingers, or like I had touched an electric fence. A quiver went right up my arm, and the line moved on again, with a sudden angry whine of the reel. I didn't know how much line I had, and didn't dare take my eyes off the river to look, but I hoped it was enough.

'Hey!' I heard the producer call. 'You got a nice one!' He started wading across.

I didn't know how he knew, yet something about the fish told me that he was probably right. It seemed heavy and powerful, yet also lazy, or tired. It hadn't shot off on some frantic course, it hadn't leapt out of the water. It had just firmly, decisively, strongly but unhurriedly swum away from me, with only one moment of wavering in the middle of the river.

The reel went quiet again. This time I managed to wind in a lot of slack line. I did it fast, in case the fish suddenly sped off and snapped the line when it hit the tension again. When I reached the weight I bent the rod back, pulling against it, heaving the beast in like a boulder, leaning the rod forwards to reel in, then lifting it backwards again like a lever to shift the heavy thing.

'Yo, dude,' the producer called excitedly, close beside me. Just then the water swirled smoothly not ten feet away. A huge tail as fat as a beer can rose out of the water and slipped in again.

'Dude!' he cried. 'You got yourself a monster. Heck. I bet that's the damn fish I was looking for. Excellent, excellent,' he added.

I wondered whether this meant I had inadvertently stepped on his patch, or that I had done him a service. Either way, he didn't seem to mind. Perhaps he was hoping to get another look at this mysterious fish, or perhaps he was biting his lip – but what puzzled me was how he could possibly know if it was the same fish anyway.

I bent the rod up again, levering the trout in till it was drifting lazily around my legs.

'Yes, yes,' the producer hissed. He pulled his own landing net from around his back and reached under to attempt to scoop out the creature. There was a flutter of motion, and domes of water broke the surface.

'Here baby, here baby, easy, easy,' he whispered, bending down to watch what he was doing, while I leaned back with the rod held aloft.

'OK, baby, OK,' he said, straightening up. 'OK, here we are, here we are.'

He lifted out the net with both hands. Lying half in it, half on it, its head and tail sticking well over either end, was a glistening, twitching rainbow trout. It worked its mouth a few times then lay still, staring at us with a target-like eye.

'Phew!' he said. 'This is a monster. A *mon*ster!'

The fish offered no resistance when I took the hook out. Then I jammed the rod under my arm and carefully lifted the beast. My two hands were not big enough to encircle it. It was slippery, soft, heavy, and I didn't raise it much. It didn't move. It looked like a fair-sized salmon.

The producer pulled out a camera from one of his many pockets and had me hold the fish in various poses. Then he held it himself and had me photograph him. His rod had inches marked off at the handle end, and we measured the fish against them. It came in at twenty-seven and a half inches.

'No,' he said. 'Incredible, just incredible.'

I was delighted with my catch, but I was tempering my reaction. I didn't feel quite comfortable about coming along on his excursion and getting the prize fish myself.

'That's gotta be eight pounds. Or nine even.' He shook his head.

'Is it the one you were looking for?' I asked.

'That one had an old hook right here.' He picked up one of the small side fins. 'Stuck there from some time when it got fin-hooked. Must have been there a long time. Didn't look like it was going anywhere without that hook.'

We replaced the fish in the landing net, holding it just below the surface so it could breathe again, with my hand on top to keep it there. Not that it felt like it was about to rush off. It didn't seem so much tired as bored by this particular ordeal, as if it knew the best thing was to lie still and let us do our stuff.

The producer turned it over, to make sure it wasn't the one he was looking for. Sure enough, there was no sign of a hook. But one of the fins had a small nick taken out of it, where it had ripped on something. I pointed this out. It was a small triangular cut, a wedge cut out of the bottom edge of one of the ventral fins.

He stooped to take a closer look, lifted the fish clear out of the water. He studied it minutely, scanning it from different angles.

'Well, I'll . . .' He shook his head. 'Heck. You know what? I think this *is* the fella. The damn hook must have pulled out somewhere along the way.' He removed his Ray-bans and bent down again. 'Whaddaya know? That beats it all.' He stood up and smiled at me. He clapped me on the back. 'Well done, partner. I think you got him. I really think you got him.'

I asked him if he would like to release the fish. He accepted, holding it under water with its mouth upstream. As the current flowed over it it began to work its gills again, slowly moved its tail back and forth, then suddenly, with a single shudder, spurted off and vanished into the dark water.

He shook my hand. 'Well, truth is I never did think I'd see that mother again. Glad to see he's doing fine. Thank you kindly, sir.'

'Thank you,' I said. I asked him what he reckoned the weight to be.

'Nine, if not nine and a half. A real monster.'

I remembered that last night he had described his mystery fish as a ten-pounder, and presumably it must have grown since he last caught it, but I said nothing. Nine sounded good enough to me.

'Back to work.' He moved across the stream. 'Let's go find his big brother.'

I laughed. 'Or his daddy.'

'Hell, I'm gonna get his grand-daddy,' he bellowed, unzipping a pocket of his waistcoat. His cry echoed within the canyon walls.

We didn't find any of the fish's relatives. By mid morning several other anglers had appeared, and it was harder to pick our spots. Before lunch the producer lost a couple of bites, which leapt out of the water and vanished as soon as they plunged back in, leaving his rod straight and light again. Then he caught a fifteen-inch brown trout.

At lunchtime we drove to a motel-cum-diner-cum-fishing store five miles downriver. It was a bleak concrete complex standing all alone in the desert canyon. The producer bought some tiny nymph flies, which the man in the store recommended, and we told him about my catch. He nodded, unimpressed.

'Last week a fellow got a thirty-one-inch rainbow. Fifteen-pound fish. Yup. There's big 'uns out there.'

We bought a cold six-pack of Beck's and drove to a dusty parking lot upstream. The producer had packed an ice-box with lunch, and we stood at the back of the car making sandwiches of smoked chicken and ham, Dijon mustard, gherkins and mayonnaise, and drank the beer. It quickly got hot standing there under the sun. I stripped down to my T-shirt, and peeled down the neoprene suit, letting my cool compressed flesh feel the warm air.

We fished till dusk, and I didn't get another bite. This didn't surprise me. I had known as soon as I got my first bite that because it had come so early in the day it might well be the last. The producer caught a fine, sleek eighteen-inch rainbow. Then when the shadows started creeping up the far wall of the canyon, filling the great trough with shade like ocean water, we made our slow way out of the river and back through the stiff grass, and changed wearily and silently by the car, dismantled the rods and slumped onto the soft seats. We sat there for a while before the producer mustered the energy to begin the drive.

As we threaded up the side of the canyon I looked back down behind us. The desert valley had become dark blue, with the river a ribbon of pearl-coloured light fallen from the sky. Darkness fell soon after we reached the top. Half-way back to Taos we switched over. I drove us down off the pine-covered mountains onto the plain. Far away, even from forty miles away, we could see the little speckling of stars that marked the town on the far side of the mesa.

The producer had to leave at dawn the next morning to catch a flight from Albuquerque. We exchanged numbers and said goodbye outside my studio. He promised to send me the photographs. Sure enough, only two days later a Federal Express van drove into the compound with a package for me. Inside were five photographs of me with the fish, and one of him. At first I didn't recognize myself, kitted out in the odd costume, grinning strangely at the camera. He had wrapped the pictures up in a sheet of paper on which he had written: 'We got him! Till the next time, when we'll get that big brother of his!'

I stuck the pictures up on the fridge door, and every time I saw that peculiar elated grin on my cheeks, an irrepressible smile rose into my face to match it, and I'd think to myself, yes, we got him, we certainly did get him.

NINE

Earthships

I FIRST SAW NATALIE GOLDBERG on the back of a book in a bookstore in Kilburn, six months before I went to New Mexico. An American friend had driven me up there on a rainy morning to buy some self-help manuals, which he believed I could use.

The shop was one narrow room, populated by raincoated figures browsing the shelves, who apologized each time they squeezed past each other. A row of umbrellas hung by their handles from a table, dripping onto the carpet. My friend pulled out books and handed them to me, filling my arms with a pile as I followed him down the shelves. They had titles like *Learned Helplessness, Living With Fear, Overcoming Indecision, More Psychotherapeutic Techniques*.

'You think I need this?' I'd ask in bewilderment each time he handed me one.

I flipped through them. In one there was a story about a girl who had been told by a fortune-teller that she would die when she was twenty-one. Six days into her twenty-second year she contracted a wasting disease the doctors couldn't identify and died a month later in hospital. That was called learned helplessness. I didn't read enough to find out how you learned it.

My friend dropped another book off for me. It was called *Wild Mind*.

'What's this?'

'She's a big hit now in the States.'

The author was Natalie Goldberg. I read the first page, then the next, and the next. As I read I had the same feeling I had had years ago when reading D. H. Lawrence at Cambridge, as if my whole body was waking up from a deep sleep. It was powerful writing and, as it happened, the author was talking about New Mexico, where she lived. She was describing walking through the streets of Taos on a quiet winter morning, the crunch of the snow, the smell of piñon smoke coming from the chimneys, the high blue sky, the black watery shadows of the plaza. It was the first morning of winter. She was walking through it, drinking it in on her way to a café called La Tazza where she was going to order a tall glass of hot chocolate with extra milk and sit at a table and take out her notebook and begin her day's writing. That was the way to live, I thought. This woman knew what life was about.

There was a picture of her on the back. She was standing out in the open air with some mountains in the distance behind her. The blurb below said she had studied Zen Buddhism for fifteen years and that her approach to writing had been informed by her Zen practice.

But what I liked was her approach to living. I skipped through the book finding the same thing everywhere: a relish for the details of life, a sumptuous appreciation of the sensuality of food, weather, buildings, bicycles, lovers, friends and friends' children. She truly loved life. She was a big-hearted woman. You could see it in every sentence she wrote. That was all that mattered, I decided: big-heartedness. Suddenly a deep yearning hit me. Life wasn't about drifting around doing jobs you didn't believe in, as I had been doing. This woman had lived as a hippie for most of her adult life, I discovered, paying a rent of fifteen dollars a month for an adobe shack high up a mountain above Taos. But she had obviously enjoyed it. I thought of her in the crisp morning air of a Taos winter, and in the syrupy warmth of a summer evening, sitting in the doorway of her shack with the mountain falling away beneath her. She had had the courage to leave her childhood in Long Island and move out west. That one step had given her so much. It had allowed her to become herself. That was what New Mexico could give you, I guessed: space. New Mexico would let you grow like a tree in the middle of a field, and support you as you walked down the street over the snow in the morning, planning only to go and sit in a café and drink coffee and write in your notebook. That kind of life was just a fantasy to me: to her, living in New Mexico, it was real.

A nauseating ache of longing for my old American life hit me. I bought the book and spent the rest of the day curled up on the couch reading it.

The next time I saw her it was in the flesh. She had just given a reading at the very same La Tazza café, which was the coffee shop next to the Taos bookstore. I was walking past one night on my way home. It was a warm night, and there was a crowd in the courtyard between the store and the café. I went in through the adobe pillars of the gate to see what was going on. I noticed her right away. She was standing at the front, beneath a patio roof, amid a circle of friends, who were all laughing. A podium and microphone stood to the side. For a moment I thought she might be about to start reading, even though it was nearly ten o'clock. But the rows of seats were empty, littered with yellow flyers advertising forthcoming events, and with a coat, a shirt, a handbag draped over the back here and there. A sheet posted on the wall of the café glistened in the light of the outdoor bulbs: 'Tonight Only: Natalie Goldberg Reads From Her New Book.'

It was odd, but all the time I had been in Taos I hadn't thought of her. All around me people were standing with glasses of cappuccino and cups of espresso with turns of lemon rind on the saucers, chattering away. I wondered what to do. I could go up and introduce myself and tell her I had loved her book, but she was surrounded by friends, and I didn't want to interrupt their conversation. While I was pondering, the crowd shifted around me. I found myself standing in a space of my own suddenly, emerging as a lone figure, like a rock on a beach when the wave retreats. I moved to the dark side of the yard, by the bookstore, and looked at the titles stacked on the table inside. There was a pile of hardbacks of a new book by Herman Wouk in a bright red cover, and a new James Michener. I shifted my focus so I could see all the people reflected in the window, looking yellow and blue in the night-time. Her entourage was still there. They were obviously having a good time. The evening had been a success. What would I say? That I had enjoyed the reading enormously? I couldn't very well lie like that.

I decided to go in and order an espresso to buy myself some time, but the café was crammed full of people. It was impossible to make out where the line was.

What the hell, I decided. I liked her book, I've seen her, I've been to Taos. Isn't that enough? Why do I have to meet her? I made my way through the crowd and went back to my studio.

But the following afternoon when I walked along Kit Carson and passed the La Tazza I regretted not having spoken to her, and went into the bookstore and asked a tall, thin man in a blue shirt behind the counter if he could give me her number.

'Excuse me?'

I asked again.

He pushed his glasses up his nose and replied in a deep voice that he didn't think they could do that.

I felt a prick of annoyance, and asked if I could leave a note.

'I don't know when she'll next be in. But sure.'

One morning a few days after that the telephone rang. A thick Brooklyn accent asked for me. It was her. She spoke slowly, heavily, suggesting I meet her in the plaza early in the afternoon.

At two o'clock I crossed the plaza diagonally, over the road and up the kerb onto the square in the middle, with its flower boxes and little brick park, wondering if I would recognize her again, and wondering also what I was doing meeting a stranger just because I had read a book of hers.

In front of the cinema on the far side next to the La Fonda Inn I saw a woman in baggy white pants and dark glasses, with a red

bag over her shoulder. She took a step forward as I approached.
'You know, I realize I only have half an hour till the movie starts,'
she said as soon as we shook hands. She was going to see *Thelma
and Louise*.

'Am I late?'

She laughed a touching, loose laugh. 'No, no. It's just that I
don't have long. Shall we just sit here in the sun?'

We sat on a bench and talked for a while. She took off her
glasses. She was beautiful, with a well-shaped, strong face, and clear
hazel eyes, and wore her shoulder-length black hair swept back
from her cheeks. There was something about the way she talked
that made you listen closely. Everything she talked about sounded
interesting and appealing. She spoke slowly and clearly – later she
told me she couldn't help talking to me as if I didn't speak English,
since I was a foreigner – and with great attentiveness. It was as if
she put her whole mind into her talking. It was something different
from most conversation. It made you feel quiet inside.

She invited me out to her house on the mesa. We arranged to
go after her movie.

I strolled back to my studio and poked the fire and picked up a
book and failed to settle down to anything. I went for a long walk,
making a big circle on the north side of town, cutting down lanes,
through parking lots, across a park, around the side of the Community Arts Center, and out onto the meadows west of town. I
got back to the plaza just as the handful of movie-goers drifted out.

Natalie lived in one of the houses made of tyres and beer cans. It
was half sunken like a bunker, and smothered in adobe. All around
stood other experimental houses – a cylinder studded with the
silver bases of beer cans like a Dr Who robot, with an enormous
two-storey plate-glass window on the south side, a mud chalet with
many odd basement additions humping up beneath the ground,
and with skylights and sloping windows cut down into the mesa,
an adobe pyramid with a heavy steel door which anyone was free

to meditate in. Outside Natalie's home a sky-blue Ford Falcon rusted with no engine. From her window you could see the top of the beer-can castle and the wind dynamo on its roof, a kind of steel hour-glass which somehow acted as a turbine and made electricity.

Her corner of the mesa was like a building site, a Mad Max encampment. Two old chrome trailers rested among a pile of petrol cans and oil drums. Now and then you would see a barefoot girl in a baggy dress cross between two of the distant bunkers, or run off after a dog with a long piece of desert straw in her hand. It was a wild place to live. From her sunken living room – sunk so when you stood up the ground was level with your chest – you could see right across the blue mesa to the mountains either way – the near Taos mountain squatting there like a Buddha at the end of a hall, or right across the blue and distantly silver land to the black rubble of western mountains on the horizon. I couldn't remember ever seeing anywhere so big and wild. It felt like if you lived here you could do whatever you wanted, whatever emerged from deep in your soul. I went out and stood on the roof for a while, which was just a hump in the sage-scrub desert, and gazed around: the huge mountains to the east, close and present on the cloudy afternoon, purple at that hour, then the hills to the south, and a flash of smoky light over in the west, and a rash of black lines just discernible in the plain marking distant gorges, then the plain itself, the sage-covered mesa reaching away to the north and west, blue far away and soft, faded green nearer. It was an afternoon of iron and lead clouds, and the whole scene from the low grassy roof looked somehow bigger, wilder and freer, more desolate, than you would think anywhere could be in late twentieth-century America. It was as if I had landed on some lost steppe of remote Asia – except that it didn't feel lonely. Quite the reverse. I felt at home.

It was an ingenious house. The beer cans and tyres gave the walls the swells and curves of a breathing beast. The adobe that covered them was a yard thick, warm to the touch with stored sunlight, and the whole floor was glazed terracotta. It seemed the most alive building I had ever been in. The walls bulged and receded, the living room was full of plants, creepers grew along the fat beams beneath the roof, and meanwhile light flooded in from the south wall, which was all glass. Even in winter the house stayed warm without any heating. The bedroom, built a little higher on the desert, up three steps, was an octagonal hall with a shiny floor, a fireplace and windows looking across the plain at knee height. There was something restful about the room, and almost regal too, in its spacious air of hushed composure.

The architect of the house, and of all the houses around, was a sculptor and mystic called Michael Reynolds. Twenty-five years ago, while meditating one morning in his homemade garden pyramid, he had been visited in a vision by four wizards. They spent all day telling him things he didn't understand but wrote down anyway. It was only years later that he managed to decipher it all, and discovered that he had been given a mission: to build homes for humans that would arrest the squandering of the earth's riches. They would be built from the very waste of modern civilization, and were to be called Earthships, vehicles for humans to travel in on their life's journey.

Natalie's house was one of the first. The other houses littered around it were early experiments he had made. Now his ideas had spread from Taos all over the south-west, and beyond. You could take weekend workshops in building your own beer-can-and-tyre Earthship. He had been on the front page of the *New York Times*.

The house was solar too. Even the pump that raised the water from her well was solar-driven. The building was connected to the rest of the world only by the telephone line and the rutted track that dipped and rose over the concealed undulations of the mesa back to Taos, eight miles away. You could see the town glittering like a spill of rubbish at the bottom of the mountains when the light was right, and twinkling like a little galaxy at night.

Natalie made tea for us and we sat at her big kitchen table sipping from coloured mugs. She showed me some of her watercolours of café scenes and farmyards and landscapes, which she was planning to put into a book, then read me some poems by a fifteenth-century Zen priest called Ikkyu. He had been abbot of a monastery, and loved to spend his nights down by the docks among the sailors and prostitutes. His moment of enlightenment had arrived one evening when he was rowing across a lake and heard a crow call.

Natalie liked the haiku-like poem in which he described hearing that caw. She read it twice, then sipped quietly from her tea.

That evening we went to Ogilvie's. We sat on the terrace overlooking the Taos plaza and ordered vegetarian burgers. It was a strange occasion. I found myself talking about things I hadn't thought of in a long time. I told her about my teenage flirtation with Buddhism, and about the time I was walking along an estuary in Ireland on a bleak afternoon and suddenly found myself weeping, right out of the blue. A sadness tinged with joy had welled up from nowhere, bringing with it memories of similar afternoons in my childhood.

Natalie nodded like she understood, and I felt that she did understand. She explained that she had taken Bodhisattva vows when she formally entered a Zen centre. That meant she vowed not to attain Nirvana until she had helped all other sentient beings reach it. She was like a shepherd who wouldn't go through the gate until all the sheep had safely passed through. It was years since I'd heard anyone talk about Nirvana, and as something actually to strive for; or rather that all beings were striving for whether they knew it or not – not only us, but also the crows, the locusts, the sharks, the cows and chimpanzees – and it made me feel good to hear it.

Natalie sat there eating the French fries piled around her burger with her fingers and occasionally took a bite out of her bun, which she had smothered in ketchup. She moved with slow deliberation. When she picked up a French fry and put it in her mouth she did it almost in slow motion, yet you felt that it was the right speed, that any faster or slower, and something would have been missing from the action.

She asked if I was planning to go to Santa Fe. If I did, she offered to introduce me to her friends down there. She had just bought a house in the city, she told me, and was planning to divide her time between Santa Fe and the Taos mesa. Sitting out there in the Taos night I realized that that would be the next phase of my trip. I had been feeling a little lost lately, wondering where to go and what to do next. I had been thinking about making the trip over to Las Vegas, New Mexico, but decided now that I would postpone it for the time being. First I would spend some time in the desert capital, the city of painters and poets.

Three Indian men from the Taos pueblo were leaning up against the wall of the terrace drinking Tecate beers with lime twists in the neck. All of them wore their hair in long black plaits. One had a red embroidered waistcoat from Guatemala, another wore a Rolling Stones T-shirt from the Steel Wheels tour. They were talking and laughing loudly. Every now and then they would glance at us. The one in the waistcoat finally couldn't resist any longer, and came over to our table.

He leaned against the edge, swaying a little, making the table-cloth fold. He smelled saltily of beer.

'Excuse me,' he said. 'You're all talking here . . .'

Natalie turned slowly and looked at him.

He faltered under her gaze, then apparently recovered his nerve and again said, 'Excuse me.' He went on: 'Why don't you-all take your niggers back to Africa?'

Neither of us said anything. I glanced at him then stared at my plate. It was hard to know what to say.

'All you got to do, just take them back where they come from.' He spoke quietly, in the soft, clipped New Mexican voice.

Natalie put down the French fry she was holding.

'Taos was a good place,' he said. 'Go back maybe four hundred years.' He chuckled, then lifted his beer bottle, which was nearly full, and tipped it right up, drinking in big hard swallows till he had finished it.

Natalie said, 'I live in Taos. Right now we're talking among ourselves and we'd like to keep on doing that. Could you leave us alone, please?'

The man gave her a salute and walked back to his friends. The three of them moved noisily into the bar to buy more beer.

I was impressed. She was like a ship travelling up a channel slowly but with enormous momentum. Nothing deflected her.

At nine-thirty she left. She had an early start the next day.

Taos changed for me after that. It was as if my encampment knew before I did that it was time to break camp. The pegs were already being clanged out of the ground with side swipes from mallets, the guy ropes were being untied, coiled up. All around me, the roof and walls that had kept me warm and dry were being slowly dismantled. I could sense the brightness of the open air now. Whatever I had meant to do in Taos, whatever I had meant to find, I had apparently done it, found it. What had been a house was now just a folded sheet of canvas. Taos was the same, yet something had gone. It was like a town on the morning after a concert when you're on tour. You walk about the streets feeling the noise and warmth and lights of the stage in your head, while what you see around you is a quiet, hollow town in the plain daylight. It is as if all secrets of the town have been bared to you.

I realized it was time to leave.

109

TEN

The Labyrinth

IT WAS LISA WHO drove me down to Santa Fe. I met her in the Plaza Bakery. She stood gazing at the notice-board right by my table. I noticed that her T-shirt was hanging out of her jeans and that her jeans were smeared with some kind of grime. At first I thought it was just grunge dishevelment, but even her shoes – black lace-ups, dusty like a tramp's – were undone. One had no laces. It looked like a severe case of self-neglect.

We got talking. It was a rainy afternoon and she had nothing to do. She invited me to come with her to the Rio Grande Gorge Bridge. She had been meaning to go for months, she said. I had been before, with Basil the student, but agreed anyway. We drove out through the rain while she played the soundtrack of the film *Paris, Texas* on her cassette. We sat in the car for twenty minutes when we reached the canyon, listening to Harry Dean Stanton singing a Latino song from Mexico, while the rain drummed on the roof and steamed on the hood. Then we drove back to my studio.

Lisa had short messy blonde hair, clear green eyes and tanned cheeks. If she had taken any trouble she could have been a great beauty. She had the facial bones of a more classical Geena Davis, of an Ingrid Bergman. She was slender and slight and seldom ate. But she was confused. She had driven out west from Pittsburgh in June for no particular reason, except to get further away from her east-coast family, and had been moving to and fro between Santa Fe and Taos all summer trying to decide where to live. She was a young art student with no plans. She wasn't even sure if she wanted to keep on painting. She had been in New Mexico two months now and the back of her car was still full of her bags, her art supplies, and a stack of pictures. She showed me some of her paintings outside the studio, setting them out on the roof of her car. They were mostly chaotic daubings, but on one, a picture of a house in winter done on a piece of board, so many layers of paint had been applied that the painting had acquired a kind of heavy, enamelled authenticity. As I studied it the shadows of the eucalyptus trees overhead brushed over it.

When I told her I liked it she made a face.

'Yeah, it's OK. But it took me so *long*. I like these spontaneous ones.' She gestured at the pile of five or six that I had leafed through.

I shrugged.

'I mean. They're so *raw*.' She pulled one out of the middle. It was predominantly yellow, the colours sketchy and thin, unfinished. She stared at it a moment. 'Why the hell *shouldn't* you do paintings fast?' She frowned. With the faint shadows playing over her tanned face and the softened sunlight making her eyes a translucent green, she suddenly looked beautiful.

'No reason.'

'I mean I hate being all anal and meticulous, going over it again and again.'

'As long as you keep on painting,' I said.

She was twenty-two. She had just finished art college. She could now do, was doing, what I had not done when I was twenty-two: headed out to New Mexico to discover herself as an artist. I wondered if I envied her, and found that for some reason I didn't.

She was looking for a house. First she wanted to live in a cabin up above Taos, but the man who was renting it lived next door, she told me, and had looked at her weirdly when he showed her round. He spooked her. Then she found a share in a house out on the Taos mesa but she wasn't allowed any overnight guests.

'So fucking parent.'

Meanwhile she was staying on the couch of a friend in Santa Fe, also an artist, so there was no immediate urgency. When she came to Taos she took to staying with me, an arrangement that suited me fine, something I took as part of the easy relaxed life of New Mexico.

It was on one of her return journeys that she gave me a lift to Santa Fe. But we didn't go straight there. She had other plans. The road out of Taos skirts the mesa, passing Ranchos de Taos with its ancient, crouching church and an old adobe hall opposite, now a bar with two blue pool tables and a 'NO GUNS' sign on the door, then the ribbon of tarmac drops down into the canyon of the Rio Grande. It is an impressive canyon, with steep, smooth sides sweeping down to the thin, white river, and we wound down one wall in a series of long hairpins. Then the road swung along from bend to bend beside the torrent.

After a few miles Lisa turned off onto a dirt track, crossed the river and doubled back on the far bank, threading through a stand of eucalyptus. 'Check this,' she said as we popped over a stretch of gravel. 'This is cool. Actually this is a place I might live. The guy has a teepee I could stay in.'

We parked in a field of rough grass below an adobe. She smiled as we walked up towards the porch. 'This is like totally cool,' she repeated. When we reached the house she brushed her hand across a set of bamboo wind-chimes hanging by the door, and knocked.

The man who answered had a cropped head and powder-blue eyes. He wore a pale grey tracksuit with the sleeves rolled up. A shell necklace hung round his neck, and he had a thong bracelet on either wrist.

'Hey, great timing,' he said. 'You ready for some coffee?' He sent me a gentle wry smile, making lines fold around his eyes.

Lisa introduced us. He was called Joel. I looked more closely and said nothing. I hadn't seriously entertained the possibility of running into the Joel I had known in Vermont, who had run off with Frankie. But suddenly I wondered if this could be him. The eyes were about right, as was his height. Could it be that Lisa had accidentally brought me to his very door? And this man was probably around the right age too, in his early forties. But he seemed too slim. The other Joel had had a certain bulk to him.

We followed him into his kitchen, which involved climbing up a set of stairs onto a raised sitting area with a view over the valley, then down a ladder into a miniature jungle of rubber plants and banana bushes. This was the bathroom, covered all over with glazed terracotta tiles. A two-foot-wide shower-head hung from the ceiling, which looked like it would release a rainstorm of water into the miniature jungle.

Was this where Joel had been living all these years? How long had he had this house? Had Frankie stayed here with him? Assuming it was him. It suddenly crossed my mind that for all I knew Frankie might still live out here too. I might be about to see her again.

The kitchen was comparatively suburban, except for an array of crystals that stood along the windowsill, on the edges of all the shelves, on top of the fridge.

He poured out three cups of coffee. I wanted to ask him about Vermont, and decided that I would begin by asking if he had been there the same year I had. But before I got my question in he said, 'So. You want to show him the closet?'

Lisa grinned. 'Right on.'

'Just a wild guess.'

She took a sip. 'Do you mind?'

'That's cool. Think you know your way around?'

She hesitated.

'I'll come along too. No problem. I wouldn't want you getting lost or anything.'

She chuckled.

He led us through a dark windowless room hung with Persian rugs to a sliding door.

'OK, you are about to enter the world's largest closet.' He fixed me with his pale eyes. 'Five years ago the hillside this house is built against started crushing the house. Some kind of subsidence. I began digging out a space between the hill and the exterior wall. I discovered I could do it with a crowbar. Or with a spoon. Whatever. It was easy. The soil is just packed sand, because the whole valley used to be a riverbed. In a day, practically, I had it all done. So I thought: wait a minute. Couldn't I use a walk-in closet in my bedroom? This room used to be my bedroom. So I knocked a hole in the wall and in a couple of days I had my closet. Just burrowed straight into the hillside. Then I thought, what the heck, why stop?' He chuckled. 'That was five years ago. I still haven't stopped. You'll see.'

He slid open the door. Inside was a large white chamber with a flat floor but otherwise without a single even surface: the walls curved upwards and met in a point thirty feet overhead, where a little disc of glass had been inserted as a skylight. Three doorways led out of the room, and above each one a plump naked woman had been carved with her thighs straddling the opening.

'This is a palace of sex,' Lisa said, and let out a high, rapturous laugh.

'It's whatever you want it to be.' He looked at her. She was gazing around the room. She threw her head back to look up at the roof, making her normally discreet bosom jut out.

The three doorways gave onto an underground labyrinth, an interminable network of tunnels intersecting here and there, snaking upwards and downwards and from side to side through the hillside. He led us on and on down his passageways. Now and then a chamber opened up unexpectedly, adorned with some piece of sculpture donated by a local artist. Here and there a tube opened off a wall. He pointed them out and told us to look through them. They all aligned perfectly with other similar tubes in chambers far away and higher up, which in turn were aligned with a skylight on the surface, so you could see all the way across a number of tunnels and chambers to small discs of sky quarter of a mile away. Some of these were lined up to offer a viewing of certain constellations at particular hours of the night. Others were aligned with a certain part of some sculpture in one of the chambers, with a head or a breast or some nodal crux in an abstract construction.

In one room he made us sit down on cathedral-like thrones that had been carved out of the sandy soil. He told us to hum. At once I heard a vibrant whine right behind my ear, as if someone was leaning in close and making the noise.

'It's the funnel shape,' he explained. The whole chamber was the shape of a bishop's mitre, and the sound waves apparently gathered at the apex and hurtled back down with a renewed collective resonance.

Another small chamber, set with a bed on a shelf, was coated in a mosaic of mirror fragments. 'This is where I want to hang out,' Lisa said. 'Smoke a joint and just hang here.' She laughed.

He nodded gravely. 'That's cool,' he said. 'You can do that.'

A couple of times we came to the end of a tunnel, where the intermittent light bulbs had not yet been installed and the smooth cement walls gave way to the sand of the subsoil. A few tools, mostly crow bars of different sizes, lay on the ground.

I was impressed. The sculptor had effectively built a work of art that could only be viewed from the inside. It was like a model of a subway system, a series of intertwined tubes suspended in a glass case; except that you could only be inside the tubes, you could never gain an exterior perspective. I had never heard of anything like it: it had no external existence at all. And it was so big, so much work had gone into it, yet it was hidden away behind a closet door, unknown to the public.

It was like New Mexico, I thought. People talked about New Mexico, and came and visited. But what it did to you, what it meant, what the place offered to the human psyche, was all incommunicable and hidden. It had its external beauty, but the real beauty of the place was in its internal effect. It opened a doorway inside you. That was what people came for. Not for the adobe houses and piñon fires and red mountains, but for what happened inside you when you were here.

Suddenly we emerged once more in the entranceway. I had no idea how we had come to it. The architect of the maze led us back to the kitchen and took our empty coffee cups. 'Got to get back to work,' he said. He was going to spend the rest of the day at one of the rockfaces.

I realized I was losing my chance to ask him about Vermont, but for some reason I felt tongue-tied and shy of raising the question. I coughed and told him I thought the construction was astounding, and I was surprised he hadn't been written up all over the place.

He nodded. 'We're keeping low for the time being. We'll open out to the world when the time comes.'

I swallowed hard and finally asked him if he had ever been to Vermont.

He stared into my eyes and nodded gently. 'Sure. I've been to Vermont.'

'Were you there in eighty-six?'

'In eighty-six?' He thought for a while, still looking straight at me. 'Sure.'

'In Stowe?'

'I've spent time near Stowe. I know Stowe.'

'Did you have a studio in that old warehouse?'

He smiled. 'You mean Jason's Mill? Sure I did. Why do you ask? You know it? You used to work there or something?'

'We've met before. Remember Frankie?'

'Frankie.' He frowned. 'Frankie.' He shook his head. 'You're going back a ways here.' He laughed gently.

It hadn't occurred to me that if it were him he might not remember her.

'What did she look like?'

'Blonde. A bit wild.'

He laughed. 'A bit wild.'

Lisa laughed too.

'Man, I need some more clues.'

'An artist from New York?' I tried. 'You drove out west with her. At least I think you did.'

His eyes left mine. He looked down at my shoes. 'No, wait. I've got it. She was kind of speedy, you might say. And aren't you some kind of fisherman or something? Right?'

He looked up into my face, beaming.

'I did it for a bit. Exactly.'

He shook his head. 'Well, what do you know. It's a damn small world. Cool.' He looked down again, absorbing the coincidence. 'What happened to her anyway?'

I laughed, a little shocked. 'I was going to ask you that.'

'We drove out to New Mex together. She stuck around a little while, as I recall. Then she left. Maybe she went off to Arizona some place. Or back east. Yeah, that's it. She went back east and got married. That's right. She sent me a card some time back. Yeah.'

So Frankie had got married.

He nodded slowly for a moment, as if lost in thought. 'Good,' he murmured. 'Good. That's fine. Fine to run into you again.' It was obvious he barely remembered either Frankie or me. Then, in a determined, rising pitch, he said, 'Well, must get back to work. Drop in again some time. That would be nice. We could hang a little.'

I walked back down to the car feeling numb. I was shocked. So that was it. I had seen Joel the artist again, seen what had become of him, and that was that. Here he was.

Lisa started up and we rocked back down the track and gradually the strange shock wore off. I began to feel good. It was good to have seen him again, seen where he lived and what had happened to him. His total freedom had set him to work tunnelling like a miner, engaged on the construction of a single work of art to which he would be enslaved perhaps till his dying day. Somehow it seemed a happy fate. His freedom had allowed him to find his perfect niche, which he was literally carving out for himself. And it seemed fitting that Frankie hadn't stuck around either. She had gone back to the east coast, where she came from, and decided to settle there. I had the sense that both their lives had settled into some kind of conclusion.

Neither Lisa nor Joel had mentioned the teepee she might live in. Once we were back on the road I asked her about it.

'He's relaxed. He knows I'll tell him when I'm ready. But I don't know if I want to stay way out here. Know what I mean?' She looked at me.

'What a place, though.'

'Yeah. But I just don't know. But hey, that's cool: you know him.'

'Kind of.'

We followed a long, empty highway to Española, a low, sprawling town with its main strip strung along the highway. Lisa told me it was the capital of low-riders, and sure enough a stream of low-riders purred slowly up and down the road, cars, mostly limousines, but also some trucks, that had been fitted with ultra low-profile tyres, with walls no more than a couple of inches high, so they cruised with the chassis a mere half inch off the tarmac. Their wheels were also excessively fat, so they projected out six inches from the body of the vehicles. They had miniature steering wheels of welded chain links, doubly power-assisted, which you could only see when someone happened to open a door. Their windows were so black you couldn't see even the faintest silhouette of the drivers.

ELEVEN

The Fat Man

IT WAS AROUND NOON when we reached Santa Fe. The first place we stopped was a deli called the Bagel Company, a tall concrete hall with wire chairs and tables, Manhattan-style. That was where I first saw the fat man. He was standing at the counter ordering when we walked in.

'Gimme a nice pound of your tunafish salad,' he was saying. He made a noise in the back of his nose. He had his hands dangling loosely by his sides, the wrists supported by the long slope of his hips. 'Then a nice pound of potato salad.'

The man behind the counter bent to the scooping.

'And some of your black olives.' His voice was soft and high, the voice of a boy. It sounded like he was about to dissolve in giggles each time he ended a sentence.

'Olives? How much?' asked the assistant.

'Oh,' he said, bringing a set of fat fingers to his mouth. 'I don't know. Whatever. You choose.'

He had no neck and no chin. The flesh started at the jaw and hung like a sheet straight down to his chest. He was wearing a blue polo shirt of tremendous proportions. I wondered where he could buy such a shirt. Who sold shirts of that triangular cut? Or trousers for that matter. I quickly calculated: if my waist was thirty-two and the diameter of a circle was roughly a third of the circumference, his waist cannot have been under ninety.

'Doctor says I shouldn't, but what the heck, I'll take a pack of those cream cakes too,' he added to close off the order.

He enunciated all his consonants with excessive clarity, chewing on the words as if they were tasty morsels. There was a grace to his movements, and that bubbling humour in his voice, as well as the plain spectacle of his girth, that made it hard to take the eyes off him. I was to see plenty more of him, but I didn't know that yet, and I was so engrossed watching him order his food that it was a moment before I realized he was done and the assistant was calling out for the next customer, which was me.

Everything he did, the way he turned round using several little steps, the way he smiled benignly at whomever his eye fell upon, the very look of him in his black-framed glasses, with the ring of grey hair surrounding his bald pate, so that above the neck he appeared to be any normal Eisenhower-generation American, perhaps a vacuum salesman or a low-range realtor, studious and resigned to his unglamorous lot – until your eye wandered down to that neck, so impossibly wide, feeding into the spherical torso – the very look of him was captivating. He possessed an extraordinary magnetism. Whether it was the faint smile that was always on his lips, or the childlike appearance of his face, which was pale and creamy, unblemished, as if he had never had to shave, he gave off an air of innocent pleasure in life, of an ability to enjoy himself every day, every hour, every moment, right at *this* moment, which was immediately alluring. There was no mistaking it: he was a powerfully attractive man.

We ordered our take-out coffees and Lisa took me on a tour of Santa Fe. The traffic was bad. We spent a good part of the trip stuck at lights on a three-lane highway that skirted town. Lisa had said it would be a quick way of getting to the east side.

'I can't believe this,' she scowled, putting her bare feet up on the blue plastic dashboard. 'It's like Boston.' (Boston was her home town.) 'In fact, I bet it *is* Boston. Half the east coast is here. I *hate* Santa Fe in summer,' she said, as if she knew it in all seasons.

It was an interesting road to be stuck on. We crawled past an old adobe church, a smoothed hulk of mud with two tremendous buttresses sticking out in front like the Sphinx's paws and a bell tower with its high mud arch looking very brown, framed against the blue sky. Most of the houses were adobe bungalows set back among piñon. They had wooden porches and shutters on the windows, all painted blue or green, and smooth corners like the church, as if pressed out of jelly moulds and made of wet sand.

Here and there stood fences made of silver plinths with stringy peeling bark. 'Coyote fence,' Lisa pointed one out. 'So Santa Fe,' she added with a note of sarcasm in her voice. But then she changed her mind. 'Actually, they're really kind of cool. I mean I'd love to have one.'

Behind them stood adobe houses with porches, all their wood-work painted in shades of green or blue, colours that went well with the adobe. They reminded me of the photograph of a New Mexican farmhouse that Frankie had shown me some years ago. Seeing house after house just like it now gave me a quiet thrill, as if I had just heard a piece of good news.

One house had a big sign attached to its gatepost. It said: 'Space Sciences Research Center.' Above was an aluminium cutout of a flying saucer.

'That's awesome,' Lisa said. She told me that northern New Mexico had more UFO abductions that anywhere else in the world.

She took me along back roads through a neighbourhood of eucalyptus trees and coyote fences and small Egyptian-looking houses. We climbed a hill to a view over town, a great roughness of lead roofs and clumps of trees raised from the plain. We stopped in at two coffee shops, one a modern place with bare plaster walls, piped Vivaldi and newspapers from all over the world, the other a simple wood house with bare floorboards and loud music and people in waistcoats, torn silk shirts and ripped jeans playing chess and smoking Camels. You could buy the cigarettes individually from a cigar box on the counter.

We drove around the blocks of downtown till we found a parking meter, then had lunch in the Burrito Company, a fast-food Mexican restaurant. I read the *New Mexican,* Santa Fe's newspaper, over my tacos, and turned to the accommodation page.

The ad at the top of the list was inviting. Stay a day, a week, a month, it said, in two luxury bedrooms in great house. Fabulous views.

I called the number from the telephone by the restrooms.

'Well, I like your voice,' the man who answered said. 'And that's a good start. Why don't you come by and take a look?' I couldn't place it but it seemed a vaguely familiar voice. He spoke with the faintest hint of desperation, as if he were having to convince me of something that seemed to him patently true. He told me his name was Ray Bryce.

Lisa drove me up there later on. The house was a sprawling adobe bungalow on a hill outside town, with a roof of large Mediterranean tiles, which gave it the appearance of a troll's dwelling, as if it had been lifted from the set of a movie of some fairy tale. An adobe wall enclosed the front garden, in which lay beds of wood chips instead of earth, nurturing nothing but piñon bushes. It was late afternoon and they had just been watered. Even from the gate their fragrance in the clear, late day was magnificent.

Flagstones led between the bushes to the thick wooden door, set with a Spanish iron grate and shutter. I could hear water flowing somewhere inside, as if someone had left a tap running. I pressed the buzzer. A peel of soft bells played a descending scale in the house.

After a moment I pressed again. Lisa switched off the car just the other side of the wall. The bells rang, the tap ran on, and the car engine ticked like a clock, then sighed. I noticed again what a fine afternoon it was, sunny and clear and aromatic. I already liked the house. Through the shutter in the door I could see a tiled lobby, and a step up to a thick blue carpet on which stood a pair of sofas. A wooden statue of St Francis guarded the lobby, and a four-tiered basket of spider plants hung above. It was a comfortable modern house and it looked cool inside, like a luxury home in the tropics.

122

No one came. Faintly, from somewhere in the house, I could hear a voice talking softly, insistently on a radio.

I rang again, then tried the door handle. It turned. I pressed the door. The seam around the rim came unstuck with a click. The door sighed and swung open a hand's width. I called. My voice fell dead among the furnishings. I checked my watch. It was five past five: I was right on time.

'Ray? Anyone home? Mr Bryce?'

The sound of the splashing water came from my right. Behind the door against the wall stood a fake waterfall, framed with rocks and moss, something you might see in an Oriental restaurant, the water trickling down in a wavering film over a blue background.

The radio was playing deeper in the house. The voice had stopped and now there was music.

I called again, waited, then went back to the car.

'Just walk on in,' Lisa advised. 'Maybe he's deaf. I mean, he is expecting you.' She was sitting with both her bare feet up on the dash, her long cotton dress hanging deep between her legs.

'Call me if you need me,' she said, pushing in a cassette.

It sounded like she knew the New Mexican protocol, so I went on through the living room, past a leather sofa and a dining table, above which hung a cartwheel with black iron lamps affixed, past a tinted-glass dresser full of ornamental plates – terracotta, elaborate Chinese glazes, Arabic brasses – to another door, which stood ajar. I knocked, then put my head round.

It was the kitchen. A brown double-door fridge stood beside a counter cluttered with blue Mexican wine glasses and old Entermann's cake boxes. The sink was piled with dirty dishes. On another sideboard stood a stack of laundered dish towels and two huge fruit bowls, in one of which a hand of black bananas clawed at the rim, and more old cake boxes. Just behind the door, draped in a blue cloth as thick as a carpet, was the table. Seated at it, with a green plate of potato and tuna salad lodged in front of him between a stained address book and a heap of telephone directories, was the fat man I had seen in the deli. He had a cordless telephone in one hand and a fork in the other.

He slowly lifted his shoulders in a shrug as soon as he saw me, and once they were up he didn't let them down. 'Well?' he said.

'I called earlier.'

He spluttered out a short laugh. He was wearing the same black-rimmed glasses as before.

'Well, sit down,' he said, his voice pitching high as if sitting down were only the obvious thing to do. 'Are you hungry? Would you like some tunafish salad?'

'No, thanks.' Something told me it was not going to be a quick meeting. 'I've got a friend outside waiting,' I told him.

'Well, bring them in. Maybe she's hungry.'

I asked, 'How do you know it's a she?'

'Oh,' he shrugged again. 'You just know.' He said it lightly, in his boylike, hoarse voice. 'But the room is for yourself, not a couple. Am I right?'

'Yes.'

'I've no objection to occasional overnight guests though. Of course not. It's your life.'

The exasperated note entered his voice again, as if he were having to convince a bigot to be more open-minded. 'No objection whatso-ever,' he reiterated. Then he tittered.

I fetched Lisa. We sat on stools around the table while Ray ate. 'So tell me about yourself,' he said between mouthfuls.

I couldn't think what to say. After two faltering starts I blurted out something about this being my first trip to New Mexico, and how much I liked it, then immediately wished I had said nothing, or tried to crack a joke. I felt my face redden.

Ray stared at me a moment, a forkful of salad poised in mid-air. He frowned with concern. 'I understand. I always wanted to come here too. We all did. You're not alone.' He lifted the fork and ate. 'I'm not from here, you know,' he added. 'I just feel like I am.'

Ray showed us round the house, pointing out his collection of sculptures of St Francis, set in niches in the walls, standing in corners, on windowsills. There were bronze ones, wooden ones, terracotta ones, ranging from thimble-sized to a life-size clay model in the back garden. 'People were smaller in those days,' he chuckled as he pointed it out. The statue, lurking between two bushes, was the size of a ten-year-old child.

One of the available bedrooms was a narrow, windowless chamber attached to the garage, the other a bright room with a thick wool carpet, a view over the hills, and a waterbed encased in a carved wood frame. A cable television stood on a small desk.

'Oh, this is the one,' Lisa exclaimed as soon as she saw it. She jumped onto the bed on her stomach and made it rock back and forth. You could hear the water slapping against the side. Ray giggled.

Either side of the bed stood white china effigies of St Francis holding a light bulb. Each bulb was covered with a clip-on leather shade.

I liked the house, laden though it was with kitsch trinkets and deep carpets and simply too many modern expensive *things*. I liked it, I felt, because Ray so obviously liked it. There wasn't a thing in it for which he didn't have a tender feeling. He rested his hand on the mattress of the waterbed and pressed it to check it was full. Then he explained how to adjust the temperature with the dial hanging from a cable. He stroked the back of the armchairs in the sitting room, set straight the Navajo rug on the leather couch, and cleared his throat as he approached the sliding glass doors that gave onto the patio in the back, before showing me how the catches worked. Then he ushered us into the yard.

The sky had mellowed to a somnolent haze, while the rugged Sangre de Cristos were bathed in a low red light that made all their crinkles and lines stand out with pellucid clarity, as if they were being seen through a magnifying glass. On the patio stood two sun-beds and a barbecue on wheels, and beyond lay a rough dry slope on which grew a huddle of piñon bushes surrounding the 'life-size' statue.

I noticed that both the sun-beds were chained to a pillar. 'You need chains?' I asked.

'Well, the first time they took both my chase lounges,' Ray said. 'So then I bought new ones and chained them to the deck table. So then they took both the chase lounges *and* the table.'

I looked at him. He paused and raised his eyebrows.

'Who?'

'We have robbers here, you know. Of course. Where doesn't? So when I got these new chase lounges I chained them up to the post like that. Now they'd have to take the whole house.' He tittered.

I politely joined in the laugh, and he immediately grew serious. 'Believe me, they'd try. There are desperate people here. The richer it gets, the poorer it gets. All the rich people moving in from LA and New York. It makes the poor people feel poorer.'

Ray's house was on the crest of a long hill. You could see the roofs of the rest of his neighbourhood spread out over the green folded land below. Higher up, the slopes rose into the flanks of the brick-red mountains.

'You know they're called the Sangre de Cristos?' he said, following my gaze.

'Sure.'

'Well, now you know why.'

I breathed in, absorbing the pine-scented evening air and the big view of the bloody mountains. 'Are they always like that? Every sunset?'

'Oh,' he demurred, lightly tapping his lips. 'Sometimes they have clouds. When they don't have clouds, I guess.'

'They always look like that to me,' Lisa said, balancing on the kerb at the edge of the patio. She lowered her toes till they touched the gravel.

Ray gave me a weekly rate and I got my bag from Lisa's car. She had to leave to walk someone's dog, she said, but I wanted her to come back later and spend the night with me in my new room. I stood with one forearm resting on the warm roof of her car and leaned down to kiss her goodbye. She smiled and turned her face up to me.

'I'll be back later,' she said. 'I'll pick you up after dark. We can go eat. I'll show you round town.'

The house was quiet. I unpacked my bag and sat rocking on the edge of the waterbed, the frame digging into my thighs. A square of yellow light lay plastered on the wall facing me, thrown in by the setting sun. I went to the window. Beyond the ornate bars the sky had turned yellow. The sun was hidden now behind a piñon bush, but I could make out the shape of the distant blue Jemez range that lay over in the west. I turned back. After looking at the daylight outside, the room seemed to be a box of soft light, a collage of orange blocks of sunshine and hazy shadows. As I looked at it a strange mood came over me. First the room struck me as very small, yet full of atmosphere. It was as if it managed to contain a great deal of light, as if it held so much soft light that somehow it must have been permeable to the outdoors, as if the force of the late sunlight came streaming right through the walls. It was good to see the room like that. My mind seemed to soften. I felt deep quiet memories stirring. I remembered the attic den I had lived in as a teenager in my mother's half-decorated house in the country-side, and how good it had been to be up there with a friend while the room, with its sloping hardboard walls, basked in the hazy shade of a summer evening. I could see us smoking cigarettes, stubbing them out in the green plastic cup we used as an ashtray. I could hear again the click of the gramophone after it finished playing a record, and feel in my nose the hot electric oily smell it gave off when it had been playing for a few hours. I could hear the note of the pigeons roosting in the houses higher up the village.

I could feel that sense of a room, a house, even a whole village being just a little thing that the elemental forces streamed over as easily as I would walk over a crack in the pavement. The sunlight, the wind, the coming of night – these things were so much bigger than our house that you couldn't even conceive of their size, except at times like this when for no reason you could explain you suddenly *felt* their size.

As I sat in Ray Bryce's spare room remembering those long summer evenings from my childhood I had the curious sense that time and space, the history of my life, the distances separating me from the various places I had lived, had been compressed. Instead of there being a thread of events that I could call my life there was only an archaeology, a layering of similar events on top of one another. Where they had occurred was as irrelevant as when they had occurred. They were all present in me now.

I wondered why I felt like this. I was evidently happy, but I couldn't exactly say why. My mood seemed out of proportion to my circumstances. For example, I was delighted at the thought that I would be seeing Lisa later, even though the time I spent with her was always a little awkward. I felt that there could be no greater good fortune than to be sitting in that little room inflamed by the sunset knowing that later on Lisa would be driving around town with me – a new town, a fragrant desert town on which night would have fallen. It seemed that nothing could ever be better than this, this sitting in a warm room in a comfortable house rich with things, waiting for dark to fall.

And I had seen Joel the sculptor again, and both he and Frankie had found lives that suited them, and settled. It was good to know that. It was as if the world was a bigger place, more accepting, than I had realized. And I was in New Mexico. That was it, I decided. I had finally come to Santa Fe. It was a smooth, suave town and there was no doubt it held some essential ingredient for the preparation of my soul. It had never occurred to me before, but now it seemed clear that my purpose in coming here was to acquire a pinch of the place, a teaspoonful of this climate, this scenery, and to use it like an alchemist to balance my unsteady soul, mixing the ingredients like chemicals in a test-tube, until they are ripe for a reaction.

I sensed something new happening to me, something outside my control. I had put my trust in my hunches about New Mexico and now a reaction in my soul was taking place. All I could do was let it unfold. There was something in me now that was as different from my ordinary awareness as that blast of orange sunset was from the little room I was sitting in. Whatever this thing was, nothing else mattered more. It had the power to illuminate every corner of my life. I had come to New Mexico without knowing quite why, and this was what I was finding: the very thing I hadn't even known I was seeking.

I sat on Ray's waterbed staring at the wall. A painting of an adobe church hung above the television. A great lozenge of apricot light half-covered the picture. Even that, the sight of a church depicted by an artist, unleashed another rush of happiness. How good it was that churches existed, that people went into them to celebrate. It seemed that they celebrated just what I was now experiencing. It was good that mud existed too, and that cool buildings could be made out of it; and that there were people who devoted their time to portraying on canvas the way they saw the world, and sharing the absorption that I was now feeling. This was the purpose of art, I decided, to share this supreme wakefulness.

I felt once again like I was being welcomed back into the world in which I belonged. It was as if I hadn't ever realized how much I was missing. I had grown used to an arid exile from myself, but now the gate was opening again. I sat watching it swing open in a daze of relief.

I wondered when this journey had really begun. It seemed clear now that it wasn't just a journey to New Mexico. It was a journey, much interrupted, much postponed, that I had been making all my life. It might have begun when I was twelve, and discovered that

I could enjoy staring out of my window at a street lamp for hours, resting on the sill, and that I loved getting up early to watch the dawn, and didn't even mind if it turned out to be a cloudy morning, a grey sky. Or when I met a Colombian priest who asked me about the people I had loved and hated and I realized not only that I had indeed hated someone, my stepmother, but also that I was capable of forgiving her, that part of me didn't mind anything she had done. Or maybe it began when I was eighteen and read *Mornings in Mexico* and for the first time discovered how prose could make you feel. Or when I was nineteen and found myself standing alone on a beach as the afternoon sun lowered over the ocean. I stared at the dazzling highway of light on the black sea and felt the boundary between myself and the water melt, so the brilliant water seemed to enter my own breast. For the first time in my adult life I recovered the familiar but long-forgotten sensation of living in a world that was not just friendly, but entirely disposed, uniquely and thoroughly *designed*, to do nothing other than support and nourish my life. Even the sand beneath my feet, fine white sand, the powdered corpses selflessly given up by countless molluscs millions of years ago just so my bare feet could stand on them – even the sand was not just an ally but an intimate. It was as if it dwelt not only on the beach but also in my breast. It was as if my breast had no boundaries, and encompassed everything I could see, or as if the external world and it were one and the same thing.

These moments seemed stages on one single journey now, and it seemed then that nothing in life was more important than this journey. What I wanted now was to find a way of not forgetting it, of making my passage through that immaterial terrain palpable, conscious, and daily.

TWELVE

Easy Rider

LISA WAS LATE. I was sitting on the terrace. I glanced at Ray through the kitchen window, and found to my surprise that he was staring straight at me. He smiled, then flapped a big hand towards his chest, beckoning.

The sky was a silky blue now, a few stars prickling it, and the mountains had become a faint, ruddy presence occupying the world. I didn't want to go inside. I waved back and shrugged my shoulders.

He beckoned again, more insistently.

He was seated at the kitchen table, with a can of dog food and a can-opener in front of him. I saw the can before I noticed the woolly black dog that sat at his feet staring up at him. Its tail twitched back and forth, impeded by the floor.

'She's hungry.' He reached a hand down and stroked the top of the dog's soft black head. 'So I wanted you to meet her. She's a new addition to the household, like yourself.'

I stooped to pat the dog's back. 'What's her name?'

'We call her Dusty. But she's only been here three days.'

The dog was a stray. She had first shown up at Ray's gate wagging her tail two weeks before. He had ignored her, hoping she would go home, but she sat by the gate patiently waiting right through the afternoon.

'I didn't want to let her in because, you know me,' he said, 'I knew I'd fall for her.' He giggled. 'You should have seen her. So cute.'

For the first time I noticed that Ray was camp. Besides being so big and having such a soft high voice and such a creamy complexion, he was also undeniably effeminate. Somehow his vastness had blinded me to it. I had thought that the way he touched his fingertips to his lips when searching for a word, the odd pitchings of his voice and his throwaway limp-wristed dismissals, were somehow all appurtenances of his size.

'And someone had been looking after her,' he went on. 'Her coat was fabulous. But she's got no collar.'

The dog paid a few more visits, scampered away each time he let her out. But since the last one she hadn't wanted to leave.

'She won't leave *me*, let alone the house,' he said, lifting his shoulders in an asthmatic laugh. 'She comes and sleeps on my bed at night.'

I wondered if that was the joke, but he continued: 'When I have company I put her on the couch.' He reached down and fumbled with her ears. The dog sat motionless, straining forwards and upwards.

'Guess where she was sleeping when you arrived? I went back just now and found her there.'

'Where?'

'On my pillow.' He wheezed, then made a sound in the back of his nose. 'But anyway, see this? I've got this fancy can-opener the can I use it?' He picked it up. 'Could you?'

It was a simple can-opener made of white plastic. I opened the can.

He sat at the table spooning the food into a plastic bowl. He did it slowly and meticulously, breathing loudly with the concentration. When the dog was chomping away at it, Ray said, 'Let's go sit in the lounge.'

He took the leather couch. It squeaked, then let out a sigh as he commenced the long sink into its cushions.

'So,' he began. 'You've been looking at me funny, like you recognize me.'

I started to apologize.

'No, no, that's OK. I'd look too if I saw one like me, believe me.' He sat very still on the sofa, which was still letting him down, until he reached bottom and sat planted there like a Buddha. 'But what I wondered is if you'd seen me before.'

Again I tried to interrupt him.

'In the movies.'

'The movies?'

'Sure. I've been in four movies. Did you ever see *Easy Rider*?'

I sat forward on the couch. It was covered with an imitation suede material, and it creaked as though there was a coat of thick plastic beneath. 'You were in *Easy Rider*?'

'Sure. Did you see the original cut? The director's cut?'

'I think so.'

'With the dealer in the black limo right at the start.'

'At the end of the runway, and that's how they get the money for the road trip?'

'Kind of. Well, I was the driver. You remember? With the fez and the Nehru coat? That was me.'

'Wow. You're a star.'

He laughed. 'And I was in the original *Fiddler on the Roof*. Topol's my good friend.' His face beamed. 'But I'm not exactly a star. Hardly.'

I congratulated him and said I'd look out for him when I saw those movies again.

'So anyway, that's why I just wondered if maybe you'd seen me before.'

Just then the dog came across the floor, a bouncy, shaky bundle of black fur. She came in a kind of slow scamper, as if a smile contorted her whole body, hampering her movements. She sat down contentedly by Ray's blue sneakers and turned her face up to him as soon as he spoke again.

'And the stage show of *Fiddler* too,' he added. 'It's still running, you know. Thirty years.'

133

I asked if he knew Dennis Hopper.

He gave a scoffing laugh. 'Who doesn't? He's always around. Always on the scene.'

'Here, right?'

'Of course. Well, Taos mostly. But he's one of the originals. He helped get the scene going, I guess you'd say. Way back, before even I got here, and I've been here for ever.'

He chuckled. 'I used to see him at parties all the time. Parties like you wouldn't believe. But that's how it was in those days. Wild, totally wild. Santa Fe was just the hottest place in America, and there were some hot places. But here —' he grimaced '— here it was a different *class* of person. Not just the stars, Bob Dylan, James Taylor and all of them, but people with something special about them.' He wrinkled his nose and rubbed his finger and thumb together. 'It wasn't just riff-raff.' Another laugh popped out of him like a bubble. 'Though Lord knows there was riff-raff too, and I wound up in bed with most of it.' He shook silently.

The telephone rang. Ray swivelled his head without moving his body. He reached an arm out for the receiver, which sat on a small black table by the couch, then changed his mind. He turned back to me. 'You'll enjoy this. I think it's Tommy.' He held out a sausage-sized puffy index finger, the other fingers curled back elegantly, and daintily tapped the speaker-phone button.

'Ray?' a gravelly voice asked in a long rise.

Ray spluttered out a laugh and plucked up the receiver, cutting me out of the conversation. 'So it's you,' he said. He smiled at me then turned to his side. He touched the lampshade on the table, turning it a little.

'Well, sure I'd like to see you. We didn't have any falling out. Not yet.' He giggled. 'Well, *sure*. That'll be swell.'

He hung up, smirking, and glanced at me. 'Just one of my tricks.'

I didn't know what to say. 'Yes?'

'Barry. You'll probably meet him later.'

The telephone rang again. Ray raised his hand over it, letting it ring three times. Right after the third ring he tapped the speaker-phone.

'Hello?' an angry voice crackled. 'Hello?'

Ray doubled up and whispered at me, 'It's Tommy. He's an old friend.' Then he bellowed, but at me, not at the telephone, 'Tommy? Is that you?'

'Of course it's me.'

'Thomas Maccaione?' Ray's eyes glittered.

'Who else?' the phone whined.

'Well, it's an honour to hear back from you.'

There was a pause. 'No one ever calls me.'

'I did.'

'First time in months.'

'Oh, how would you know?' Ray said with mock impatience. 'You're always too busy out painting. You're never there to take a call.'

The voice mumbled something.

'What?'

'You can always find me on Canyon Road,' it said.

'Still painting?'

'What kind of a question is that?' There was a pause. 'So who have you got there? You're not alone, are you?'

'A very nice English friend.'

'I never see anyone these days.'

Ray's eyes twinkled. 'Well, maybe *we'll* come and see you tomorrow. Tomorrow morning. We'll bring you coffee.'

There was a grumble for a reply.

'You'll like my friend. Just your type,' Ray added, and broke up in a wheezing laugh.

There was another indistinct reply and the caller hung up.

'Who was that?'

'You mean you haven't heard of Tommy Maccaione? You didn't even see his billboard on I–25?'

135

Interstate 25 was the highway from Albuquerque to Santa Fe and on north to Colorado.

'Let me see.' Ray tapped his lips. 'The billboard says: "Thomas S. Maccaione for Mayor." Mayor of Santa Fe, that is. "Messrs Picasso, Monet, Van Gogh Stand Aside for the New Star of the Art World Firmament." That's right. "Art World Firmament."'

'What's it all about?'

'Tommy's a painter. He's kind of famous, too. He paints on the street. Always the same street. Canyon Road, where all the galleries are. He thinks the Mayor of Santa Fe should be an artist since there are so many artists in town.'

'Are there so many?'

'*Sure.*' Ray squeezed out the word, frowning. 'Santa Fe is just full of artists. That's why people come here, to be artists.' He giggled. 'Or else to find love.'

'You mean they just come and hope to turn into artists?'

'You don't think they come here to be accountants or realtors? God knows there are enough of those everywhere else.'

Ray sent me to get a soda from the fridge. The little dog got up, scampered after me towards the kitchen panting happily, then changed its mind and went back to Ray.

'So how long are you staying?' he asked when I settled again.

I told him I wasn't sure, and for the first time it struck me that I could stay longer than I had originally planned. Already I had been in New Mexico for four weeks. My flight back was booked in one week's time but I could always change it. It hadn't occurred to me before.

He said it was OK if I didn't yet know how long I'd be in the room. 'Just let me know when you make up your mind, that's all.'

I wondered if I might even decide to live in Santa Fe.

Lisa arrived at nine-thirty. She hit two little beeps on her horn and kept the engine running.

'There's a great band at El Farol.' She was wearing exactly the same clothes as when I last saw her: a long baggy green dress which buttoned up the front, made of a light pyjama cotton, and frayed sneakers. When I leaned over to kiss her I caught a whiff of stale sweat, and for some reason didn't mind, even though I had just showered and changed.

She drove us to the plaza first. A few couples, tourists in white shorts and T-shirts, strolled around window-shopping at the boutiques and gift stores. The town was quiet for such a popular little city and for such a balmy desert night.

We hissed up a narrow street between two adobe walls, past a plush new adobe-fronted hotel and along a small tree-lined river sunk in a gulch, then followed a lane that meandered uphill, flanked on either side by small art galleries. This was Canyon Road.

El Farol was an old south-western bar. In three plain rooms at the back they served Spanish tapas and in the main bar a rhythm and blues band was rocking through Eric Clapton's 'Cocaine'. The bar was lined with men on stools. A native American with straight black hair down his back was busy drawing on the back of a take-out Chinese menu. Next to him a man with a grey ponytail and crimson waistcoat on his otherwise bare back was busy chatting to the bar-maid, prolonging his ordering of another shot of José Cuervo, while beside him two men in button-down shirts and black moustaches leaned close together as they talked, stamping rings on the bar with their beer bottles.

Lisa and I stood behind them and drank Dos Equis. Then she wanted to dance. You could feel the old floorboards sagging beneath the weight of the crowd. It was a long time since I had danced to such old music. It took me back to my early teens. Most of the people on the floor were in their forties or more, and they shook their heads to the beat like old rockers, hooking their thumbs in their belt loops. The band reeled off one early 1970s hit after another: Creedence Clearwater Revival, Ten Years After, Eric Clapton, Alvin Lee – all the great old rockers got a look in.

After the set the guitar-player chatted to me at the bar, having heard my accent. 'I was playing with a limey just two weeks ago,' he said. He was a short tubby man with a grey moustache. 'Too bad you weren't here then. You'd have enjoyed that.'

'Who was it?'

'Keith,' he said, resting his chest against the bar and swigging from a bottle of Corona, one boot hooked on the brass rail below.

'Not the Keith?'

He raised his eyebrows. 'There is only one Keith. Right?' He glanced at me. 'He comes through town now and then. Always jams with us when he does.'

I couldn't believe it. I had stumbled into the playground of my childhood heroes, my only real heroes.

'Does Mick ever come?'

He laughed hoarsely. 'Everyone comes to Santa Fe. All you've got to do is sit tight. They all come. Can't stay away. It's the Land of Enchantment.'

'Land of Enchantment' is New Mexico's state moniker, just as New Jersey is the 'Garden State' and Wisconsin 'America's Dairyland'.

He took a swig from his bottle. A deep double dimple appeared as he drank. His cheek looked grey, grizzled like his hair from an interminable rock and roll lifestyle.

Down the bar I saw that the native American with the fine head of shiny hair was deep in conversation with Lisa. He seemed to be explaining something to her, illustrating it with a sketch on a napkin. Lisa caught my eye and beckoned.

'Check this,' she said. 'This is cool.'

The guy had a mapping pen in his hand. Very fast and accurately he was drawing a detailed picture of an eagle, a mosaic-like image made up of hundreds of little lines. It was simultaneously realistic and mythical-looking.

'Sky eagle,' the artist said, drawing in the second talon. The menu I had seen him drawing on earlier lay by his elbow. I could see part of the drawing he had done on it, and it seemed to be the same eagle image.

'Is it a totem?' I asked.

He carried on drawing, and without turning round said, 'Power animal.'

'Cool.' Lisa leaned to the side to watch his pen-work.

'Yeah,' he agreed. 'Real cool.'

He wore three big silver rings encrusted with turquoise on his drawing hand, and I noticed that the leather jacket draped over his stool had the same eagle design emblazoned on the back. He seemed to be a cross between a shaman and a heavy-metal biker.

'Great helper,' he went on, chuckling.

'Yeah?'

'Sure,' he said, long and slowly. 'Big helper, the eagle.'

'Sounds like you know the eagle well.'

He laughed. 'We go back,' he sighed. 'Long ways.' He spoke in that same clipped quiet voice I had heard elsewhere in New Mexico. 'My granddaddy's granddaddy and *his* granddaddy's granddaddy.' He laughed again, a heavy ungainly laugh. 'Eagle helped them all.'

'Were they shamans?'

He became serious. 'Show me the man who isn't a shaman.'

Lisa said, 'Right.'

I swigged from my beer, getting only half a mouthful, all that was left. I put it down and rested my elbow on the bar ready to order another. I offered the artist a drink, which he accepted, then asked his name.

'Sky Hawk. Yeah. But most people call me Rocket.'

'Rocket?'

He laughed.

'Where'd you get that name?'

'Nam, I guess.'

'You were in Vietnam?'

Again the laugh. 'One tour.' He nodded. 'I was bad.'

'Is that why they called you Rocket?'

'No. That was something else. Heh heh. They called me Rocket in Pocket.'

He stopped laughing abruptly and shrugged his shoulders. 'There.' He put the top on his pen and slid the napkin with the new eagle picture along the bar towards Lisa.

'I can keep it? Cool.' She folded it and put it in a back pocket in her dress.

The band started up again. We shouted out some more chat with Rocket in Pocket then went back to the dance floor where the same crowd had formed again, and danced till late.

Ray had given me keys. Just as I put the key in the door a peal of laughter came from inside the house. Ray was still sitting on the leather couch where I had left him, but now he was wearing a pair of check boxer shorts and a tight white T-shirt. A black-haired youth, Hispanic, sat beside him. Another man who looked in his thirties, with wiry ginger hair and a ruddy face, was perched on the arm of an armchair. He was the one I had heard laughing. He laughed again now, just after we entered the room.

Ray was beaming and shuddering silently. His cheeks and the top of his head were bright pink. The youth sat in silence. There was something about the way the three of them were sitting there late at night, one so huge and half-undressed, one laughing away like that, and the third morose, that made me uneasy. I was glad Lisa was with me. I hoped we could slip quietly by with a brief goodnight.

But Ray saw an opportunity for fun.

'Barry,' he roared at the ginger-haired man. 'Stop laughing. Stop being so rude. Meet my new guests.'

Barry did stop laughing, and looked at us, but there was a bright glint in his eye and I could see he wasn't really taking us in. He was still amused by something. For some reason I particularly didn't want to know what the joke was, and feared that at any minute they would tell me.

'So, Barry, this is Henry and Lisa. And this is Jim.'

The young man with the black hair glanced at me then looked away.

'Say hello.'

He mumbled, 'Hello,' in a deep soft voice. He was good-looking, hardly into his twenties.

'You're terrible,' Ray said. 'I ask you into my home and give you drinks and I don't know what-all and you can't be civil to my friends. You're just like all the other tricks.'

Barry said, 'Oh yeah?'

'Well, not exactly the same.' This made them both guffaw still more emphatically. Jim said nothing, a mop of his fine black hair lying over his forehead. He blew from his bottom lip and made it jump. It settled back down in the same place, then he blew it again.

'So?' Ray said to him.

'So?' he murmured.

'So say hello.'

'I already did say hello. God.'

Now he looked younger still, perhaps even in his teens. He was wearing a pair of hi-tech black and white sneakers, jeans, and a white tank top. He sat very still with his feet planted squarely on the floor.

There was a moment of silence. Then Ray said, 'What?' He said it in a new voice I hadn't heard before, a voice that even though it was very similar to his normal speech seemed to come from an entirely different person. It was high, it was even soft too, just as usual, but instead of carrying a note of friendly enthusiasm it seemed to issue from someone who had only ever felt bitter and callous.

'What?' he snapped again, in an even colder tone. There was a grating edge on the word now.

Jim apparently knew what was coming. 'Oh, God,' he said, shaking his head. 'I was just saying that I did say hello to these folks.'

141

'What?' Ray barked. He was still sitting in exactly the same posture, had the same round physique, the ring of grey hair at the back of the head, the Sergeant Bilko glasses, but now instead of looking harmless he had become a ball of venom. Fury, an icy vindictive rage, seemed to have possessed every cell of his body. You could see it just by looking at him. He had turned into somebody dangerous, somebody to treat cautiously, to avoid.

'You don't show up when you're supposed to, you call up with some story about I don't know, your *mother* again, as if you care about your fucking mother, I have to come out and get you, you make me get out of the house in my condition, and then you make me get like this, you do *this* to me, you know what the doctor says, you were here last time he came, you heard what he said.' He paused. 'And don't forget I know all about Osco's, I know exactly what you did there. You better be careful or I'll have you put away again, right back inside, and I only ask you to be *civ*il and you can't do it.' Ray shook as he spat out the words. I had never heard anyone inject so much vitriol into a speech. Every word came out in a suppressed icy growl, in the voice of the wolf in a children's play.

Jim rolled his eyes and blew his hair up again. Lisa touched my shoulder. Barry slid off the arm into the armchair. Ray stared at Jim.

'Well?'

'Well?' Jim returned, not looking at him.

'Well, what do you say?'

Jim did not reply. Ray rephrased the question. 'What have you got to say for yourself?'

Jim shrugged and looked at the door.

'Doing this in front of my guests.' Ray was talking without the venom now, in an even, unfriendly tone. 'Well?'

Jim sighed, accelerating the end of the sigh to flip his hair. 'I guess I'm sorry,' he muttered. He made a sound that could have been a laugh.

Ray smiled. With that one smile his entire bulk seemed to restore itself to its former cheerfulness. 'Good. So that's over.'

I said, 'We're just on our way to bed.'

'As you like.' Ray shifted on the couch for the first time, staring at me with his bushy eyebrows raised high over the frame of his glasses. 'And don't mind us. If you close the door you won't hear us. And we won't hear you either.' He emitted a chesty titter.

Barry joined in with a grating repeater laugh, which followed us down the hall and was still audible as a soft pattering after I closed the door. He seemed to go on finding it funny a long time, and all that time, as long as I could hear him, I kept on seeing the last thing I had seen before leaving the sitting room: Jim sitting there in silence with his hands cupped together in his lap in the owl-hoot position. I could see he was fighting not to lift his hands up and try a note.

'What's Osco's?' I asked Lisa, while I experimented with the rock of the waterbed.

'I guess it's a store, a drug store or a grocery store or something.' She started rocking too, making the water slap up hard against the headboard. 'This is cool.'

'A store? He must have done a store.'

'I guess.'

'And he's been inside. How old do you think he is?'

'Younger than me. Eighteen, maybe nineteen.'

I thought back to my life at that age. A pang of regret hit me. I should have gone to work in a mine, or on a ship, found some kind of life that would have suited me, instead of stewing in the libraries of a rainy town. I should have gone out and held up some stores.

But the regret couldn't find a foothold. A tender feeling rose in its place, not for myself but for Jim, who was probably still sitting on the couch next door enduring the jokes of the two older men, saying nothing, but for some reason waiting in silence until something allowed him to leave. It looked like he would be staying the night. I wondered about his life, where he came from, who his mother was, what she did and where she lived. He was evidently short of cash. I thought about his future. I could only see him tripping himself up as he tried to run ahead, and falling into the arms of the law again. It was sad. It was sad, too, that he was in this house now, tied in some way to the enormous man next door. He seemed a beautiful young man, but doomed.

THIRTEEN

The Rock of Unknowing

THE CURTAINS WERE OPEN, and at the first paling of the sky I awoke into one of those pools of lucidity that a mild hangover can bring on. I looked at the clock: five-twelve a.m. Lisa was lying with her head thrown back and her mouth open. I could see the sky outside, a deep clear blue, the blue of some crystal in a test-tube. The sight of it snapped me into perfect wakefulness, a mood of calm mixed with anticipation, a mood not to waste on trying to get back to sleep.

Ray had mentioned a bicycle in the garage. I let myself out and crept round to the garage door.

There was no handle, no way at all of opening the door from the outside. I stole back into the sleeping house, with its low hisses and ticks and thrummings, crossed the deep and now cool carpet in the living room, and opened the door into the garage. It was dark, except for a line of pale blue light lying beneath the main door. The bike, an old racer which Ray said he no longer used, which he could hardly have used for a number of years, stood leaning on its stand at the far side of a Honda saloon. The chain was rusty – it gave off that bleachy, tannin-like smell of rust when I spun the pedals – but it was roadworthy. The tyres were hard.

It was an electric garage. I had to hit the upper button on a console attached to the end of a thick cable, take the bike outside, then go back in to hit the lower button and duck out into the open air again before the door closed me in.

It was the perfect end to a night. The street lamps of Ray's neighbourhood were still on, but a clear, weak light suffused everything, like evening twilight but more watery, like a vapour, an alcohol. It made the pine-quilted hills seem vaporous too, soft green clouds with the lamps glowing here and there among them. The bicycle wheels hummed on the new asphalt and the chain clicked as I free-wheeled down the hill away from the driveway, circled a tight bend and dropped onto the main road, which ran just below the crest of the ridge, and sailed down the long hill into town.

The clock on the Scottish Rite Temple on Paseo de Peralta said five-twenty. I cycled round the Paseo, past the low adobes with their blue porches, and made a left at the lights on Palace, heading eastwards out of town along the straight wooded road.

After a mile I made the turn onto Cerro Gordo, a narrow road that threads up the side of the valley east of town. I climbed between small eucalyptus trees, pedalling heavily, until the road became a dirt track. It had formed into natural corrugations. I had to ride slowly. A layer of white dust lay on the ribs, banked up here and there by tyre marks into long, thin dunes. But there was no traffic, it was fresh out in the open air, and it was good riding.

I cruised aimlessly for a while, killing time, taking any turn that looked inviting. Most were dead-ends. I would wind up to where the track ended in a heap of rubble by the last house, then roll back down again. Up at the cul-de-sacs where you came face to face with the natural landscape, the scent of piñon was strong, a keen spice on the morning air. Below I would see the land undulating beneath its dark-green coat, and here and there a wall of adobe, a lead roof, the gleam of a car's bumper.

From above, Santa Fe seemed like a relaxing, simple place to live. All the time you would have that desert right outside your window. It would be easy to lead a pure, productive, honest life here. I fantasized for a minute about living here myself, what kind of car I would drive, what kind of house, how near town, who my wife would be. Then I remembered the time.

It was five-fifty when I walked the bike down a gravel track and left it leaning against a coyote fence, then followed a path past an apple tree and knocked at a wooden door. The two beats sounded out clear in the dawn. A woman opened the door wearing a black robe beneath which a pair of grey tracksuit bottoms and white socks showed. She smiled and gestured me in without looking at me.

I smiled back and entered, feeling somewhat abashed by her averted eyes, wondering if there was something about my face she didn't like. She closed up, then led me through a courtyard, in the middle of which stood a Tibetan stupa. She paused and bowed when she was half-way round it. I imitated her, making a brief bow with my palms together. It was a fine little courtyard, paved and immaculately clean, its adobe walls thin and delicate, and a delicious colour, somewhere between orange and grey and rose, against the twinkling dawn sky.

At the far side we paused again by a low door. The woman pointed at five pairs of shoes lined up on a bench. I smiled at her, not understanding. The shoes were a mix of sneakers and boots. She still wouldn't look at me, and I wondered if she meant I should select a pair.

She nodded at them again.

I got it, and sat down to pull off my boots. While I was doing it she bent close and finally spoke to me, in a hoarse whisper that smelt of stale cloves and sleep. 'Have you sat Zazen before?'

I hesitated, glanced at her. She was staring at my socks.

'No.'

'Take one of the black cushions. I'll instruct you.'

Suddenly I felt my first twinge of doubt, or rather fear. It was Natalie Goldberg who had told me about this place, the Santa Fe Zen Center, and their daily morning service. I had been thinking about coming to check them out. This morning had seemed the perfect time, when I had spontaneously woken up early enough anyway. But what if they were all kooky? What if it was some cult? The way she wouldn't even look at me made me uneasy. And I had heard that in Zen halls you weren't allowed to move, not even to scratch an itch or wipe a running nose. If you did, some prefect came and hit you with a stick. The impulse that had brought me here was deserting me now, just as I was about to enter and most needed it.

She pushed open the little door and we ducked into a vestibule. From this another door, weighted with a piece of iron on a rope to hold it shut, led into the hall itself, which was a small, square room, painted white, with a large window giving onto the courtyard. A candle flame glowed steadily on a little altar against the far wall. Not a breath of wind seemed to stir in the room. A stone Buddha and a single carnation also stood on the altar, which was nothing but a piece of pine board. Otherwise the room was unadorned.

Five people were already in there. They all wore the same black robes as the woman, and sat on the floor facing the wall, three on one side, two on the other, each on a black mat with a cushion on top. Their legs were hidden by their robes, but it looked like they might have been sitting in the lotus position. Several other places lay vacant along the walls.

I immediately had two distinct reactions. One was fear that I would be expected to sit in the lotus, which I knew I couldn't do. The other was a sense of peace. The silence in the room was absolute, and the stillness so strong that it seemed nothing could have disturbed it. All at once I became conscious of the hissing of my ears, and of an eager anticipation in my chest. It seemed the cleanest room I had ever been in, and the prettiest.

The woman pointed me to one of the cushion sets. She knelt very close to me and asked in a breathless whisper, hardly allowing the air to escape from her lips, 'Can you sit in the half lotus?'

I didn't know, and tried it.

She said, 'Good.'

I had one foot jammed on the opposite thigh, pressing so hard into the muscle it hurt, while the foot itself was twisted up at an impossible angle. It wasn't good at all. I wondered if my ankle would snap.

She told me how to sit, with the back very erect, positioned my hands correctly, then instructed me on counting off my breaths in groups of ten.

'Is that all?'

She nodded. 'And be still. Try and do one period,' she breathed.

I felt the fear rise into my throat again, realizing she was about to leave me and I was really going to have to start, and not just start but keep going. Ever since I sat down I had felt a sneeze coming on.

'How long is a period?'

'Thirty-five minutes. You'll hear the bell.'

I leaned close to her without losing the posture and put my lips right against her ear. Hardly voicing the words, just letting the consonants form their miniature clicks and smacks and hums, I said, 'Can I blow my nose?'

I leaned back to let her give me the reply.

She whispered, 'Let it run.'

I heard her rustle away to the other side of the room. There was a pause, then more rustling as she settled herself. Then all was still again. I heard someone swallow.

It was dark in the room, but I could see the shadow of the person next to me quivering on the wall as the candle flickered. Nothing else moved. After a minute a ping sounded from behind me. Someone had silently struck a bell. It was a clear, high note, and you could hear it a long time, till it faded into the hiss of silence. Then it came again, ringing until you weren't sure if you could still hear it, the sound seeming to reappear as the sun sometimes does just after it has set. The ping sounded for a third and final time. Someone cleared their throat.

Strange things began to happen.

First my chest became tight. It felt like someone had strapped a belt round it. Then my ankle burned, and my thigh, then one of my knees. My nose became cold, as did the skin beneath my nostrils. It was a sensation I hadn't had in years: that of not wiping a running nose. Slowly the coldness travelled down onto my top lip. Then I tasted it in my mouth. I tried to ignore it and start counting my breaths, but I found myself suddenly concerned for Ray's bicycle. I hadn't thought twice about leaving it outside unlocked, but now I wasn't sure it was safe. What would I do if someone stole it? Should I get up and bring it into the courtyard? But the courtyard didn't seem the kind of place you could leave a bike. Then at least to the inside of the coyote fence? But could I get up? If I couldn't even wipe my nose surely I couldn't stand up and leave the room.

I decided I would have to postpone making a decision on this for a while. Until then I would try to do the breath-counting exercise. Perhaps that would calm and relax me enough so I could make a good decision. Perhaps I would get into a state of mind in which all the other meditators would sense that I was acting perfectly, with flawless intention, if I did get up and leave the room. Perhaps I would manage to do it in such a way that I would only deepen their meditation and understanding.

Meanwhile a cold line now lay over my chin. I could tell that the drip had cut loose and was dangling like a spider on the end of a thread, swaying some way beneath my jaw. I wondered how long it would be till it extended itself into my lap, and if I would be able to stay still enough for it not to swing against my shirt.

I started trying to calculate how long it took me to breathe ten times so I would know how many cycles I had to count to fill half an hour. Suddenly it seemed that I had been sitting there for much longer than that already. Whoever was supposed to have struck the bell to end the period must have dozed off. I panicked. Was someone going to alert them to their error? If we were all obliged to sit still who could do it? Would I have to? But I didn't even know what time we had started.

Just then an acute pain illuminated my right knee. It was an absurd pain, an excessive pain, ridiculously sharp. It was obvious that I would have to move the leg. Twice I leant a degree away from it, which didn't help, and considered lifting it, straightening it out and sighing with relief. But twice I stopped on the brink of moving, and the pain came back worse than before.

I wanted to groan and cry out, and could hardly believe that I wasn't allowed to. For a moment it seemed incredible, preposterous, somehow patently false, that I should have to sit still enduring this pain. It was undoubtedly damaging my leg. Pain was after all a healthy warning signal, a valid piece of wiring in the body alerting you to danger. It was absurd to ignore it. It got worse and worse. It seemed that my knee was very hot, then very cold, then a blade was cutting into it, then a high-voltage current. A couple of times I tried in vain to follow my breaths and count them, but never got past number two. The panic grew. I was ready to run screaming from the room and lie gasping in the courtyard like someone who has been in a steam bath too long. I tried to remind myself that I was just sitting on a cushion in a meditation hall. I was perfectly safe. But I felt in danger.

Intense self-pity seized me. I could feel my eyes beginning to water. It was just then, as the image of the candle-shadows on the wall blurred in my eye, that I became aware of a new sensation. It felt like I had become a cave inside. Suddenly I was not sitting in a dark, quiet room, I myself *was* a dark, quiet room. It was as if my midriff had opened out into a hollow, and in the hollow a low candle flame was burning. It made the panic turn into another feeling, one of warmth and peace and above all a yearning, joyful love, as if I was in love with someone. For a moment I tried to figure out who this might be, and realized the feeling pertained to no one. I was just in love. Even my legs had stopped hurting. The pain in my knee had vanished. Now it just tingled and felt warm. It was as if currents I hadn't ever been aware of were circulating all around my limbs, connecting the different parts of my body in one easy circuit.

151

I couldn't understand it. It crossed my mind that this might be correct meditation. It felt like I had slipped through a gate and was sitting in a new land, where all was calm. Suddenly my thoughts seemed to have stopped. In their place there was a rich peace, both in me and around me. In the midst of it, my breaths slowly came and went. It was easy to follow them. I stayed like that for a while, feeling packed full of stillness, floating in the midst of stillness. Very soon, much too soon, it seemed, a clear, light bell-note sounded. It was a very soft sound, like a smooth singing voice. I sensed it as much in my belly as in my ear. It grew low then sounded again.

I heard a faint rustling beside me and noticed that the shadow on the wall had moved lower. The person next to me was bowing. Out of the corner of my eye I could see that he had his hands together in the prayer position. I did the same. The shadow was also blurrier, greyer, and I realized that the room had grown brighter. The sun must have risen outside. There was more rustling as everyone stood up and rearranged their cushions, setting the round one in the middle of the square and sweeping them both off with their palms. Then we all stood facing the middle of the room and somebody hit two wood blocks together. We bowed once more.

The period was apparently over. This, I assumed, was my moment to leave. But now I didn't want to leave. The person with the wood blocks, whoever it was, struck them again and we all turned and shuffled a few paces till we stood in a single file looping round the little hall. We stayed like that for a while, till I noticed more faint rustling sounds and saw that the person in front of me, whose back I was facing, had taken a tiny step forwards, not more than half a foot. I did the same. Then the woman in the tracksuit bottoms was at my elbow, inhaling sharply and telling me to fold my hands on my stomach and take half steps.

'Walking meditation,' she whispered. She had apparently forgotten her suggestion that I leave after one period. Or perhaps this was all part of the period.

We shuffled slowly down one side of the room, turned the corner and made our way along the next, like a procession of monks. Our shadows shifted across the floorboards, the robes made barely audible whisperings, and as we moved the light played strange tricks on the eye, suddenly growing bright, then very dim, then hazy, then sharp. But it felt good to walk slowly. After a few paces the same sense of all-pervasive peace returned. It seemed blissful to be able to step slowly round a room just after dawn, with a group of people intent on ushering all living creatures into the state of Nirvana. There was nothing to think or worry about; simply nothing except this slow, measured walk, the rustling of the robes, the shifting of the shadows, and the knowledge that outside the window there was a bright, high New Mexico sky, as we glided through the twilight of the Zen hall.

Then the wood blocks were sounding again and we were all back at our places, settling down for another bout. The bell rang as before, and the stillness resumed. But I lost the feeling of peace soon. The ache in my legs came right back and I found myself once more panicked about it, and about Ray's unlocked bicycle outside. Various other pressing concerns lined up to present their cases too: I should be thinking about how long I was intending to stay in New Mexico, and whether I still had any intention of trying to find the Flying Father over in Las Vegas, and whether I would come to this meditation hall every day, and whether I would stay on at Ray's, where the prospect of somehow getting tangled up in his odd gang was alarming. And meanwhile the pain in my knee started up again. But it didn't receive the same miraculous relief as last time. I waited for it, expecting it any moment like a drug high, but it never came. Instead I just got more and more anxious, wondering what kind of permanent damage the searing pain must indicate, feeling myself trapped in a slow self-mutilation.

When I tried to stand up at the end I fell over. Both my legs had gone dead. No one noticed. I put my hands on the floor to hold myself upright and used the wiping off of the cushions as a pretext for keeping low. As I straightened up a second time the blood suddenly shot back into my legs, like a bucketful of warm water tipped into two hollow tubes. My limbs tingled and sparkled while I balanced there, feeling myself planted on two scintillating poles of energy. I was the last one out. As I left I saw someone kneeling at the altar, cleaning it, lighting up a fresh stick of incense.

It was sunny outside, and Ray's bike was waiting where I had left it. I didn't want to go straight home. I felt good, like after a long swim or a hard bout at the gym. It might just have been relief at being free to move again, I thought, but it seemed more, as if I had just wrestled with some monster and got the better of it, and somehow purified myself.

I rode back into town first, then up through 'Rancho Encantado', a new neighbourhood adjacent to Ray's, passing low comfortable-looking homes with Nissan and Toyota all-terrain vehicles parked in their driveways, taking my time. The morning air still had the chill of night on it, like fruit taken from the refrigerator to the breakfast table, and the hillsides were deep in the shadow of the mountains. It was after seven now, but the world still carried the watery clarity of the end of dawn. Some lights of the neighbourhood were even burning still, embedded among the houses of red earth and among the green piñon like pearls sewn in a cushion. The world seemed a soft upholstery.

I stopped beside one house, intrigued by a miniature windmill that stood at the end of the drive. It doubled as a mailbox. The message 'The Kasslers' had been painted in bright red on the side. It was a model of a western cowboy wheel, a flimsy pylon with a fan and tail on top. There was not a breath of wind and the sails stood motionless.

I was still glowing from the Zen centre, and I felt lucky like a child with a new toy, or with the kind of pet I had fantasized about having as a child, one you could keep in your pocket and take with you wherever you went. I looked at the little windmill and noticed a shiny green beetle on one of the sails. It was crawling slowly towards the hub. I stooped, leaning the bike close, and watched the little thing studiously travel along the rough board. I wondered whether it would have realized if the mill had been turning. Would the rotation have made any difference to it? Did it have any idea, for that matter, what kind of extravagant object it had landed on? I thought of Aristotle, who said that though we may not like a beetle in the flesh, we enjoy seeing it represented in a painting. He had been trying to explain the human love of seeing things represented in art, but he was still wrong, I thought. It was wonderful to watch a real beetle on a fake miniature windmill in the early morning in New Mexico.

I decided the beetle had no idea what it was on. It had no need to know. There was something touching about its bumbling ignorance, its blind faith. It was on something, and all it had to do was keep going. As I watched, a feeling grew that all creatures were somehow no different. I felt that I too went about my business without realizing I had alighted on something vast. Coming into life was like the beetle's alighting on a driveway, a roadside, a tree. We were all little creatures dwelling on something vast and unknowable, a great rock of unknowing. Perhaps this was why mankind had spent so much of its history wandering – we moved about in the hope of finding some clue to the nature of the vast thing, whatever it was, that supported us all. If we found no explanation here, perhaps we would over there, or there, or there. We crawled across the land the same way the beetle crept along the miniature sails of the model windmill, examining it for some crack in its solidity, some spy-hole through which we might catch a glimpse of something beyond or behind it, some hint as to its real identity.

The beetle climbed on to the iron bolt in the middle of the wheel, stopped, and began its journey along the opposite sail. It paused when it reached the tip. I could see its antennae feeling the edge of the wood. It was debating whether or not to turn the corner on to the flat, thin end. But before it tried, before it even had a chance to make up its mind, two doors opened in its back, flipping out like two ungainly turtle's flippers. It hung there in this new form for a moment, until the wings flicked out, already buzzing, and with a shaky movement it flew away low over the road, swaying heavily from side to side like a drunk on a bicycle.

I watched it go till my eye lost it. As I stared I felt relieved and somehow nostalgic at the same time. The beetle seemed to take something away with it, as if something was ending. I found myself thinking about my family suddenly. I missed them. When I was in England seeing them was no thrill, but now, far away, I yearned for them. I felt sad, too, that my family had broken up. I was only seven at the time it happened, but I wondered now whether all the travelling I had done had been in part an attempt to escape from that early grief, a misguided search for the father who used to live in my home. I had been playing with the idea of staying longer in New Mexico, but now the thought crossed my mind that this might be the first trip I had ever made which was turning out a success. It might make no sense to travel any more afterwards. I wasn't just homesick now, but eager to ride on into my life at home, to conquer any ancient sadness that obstructed me. If you wanted to get to know a rock, there were two things you could do: either examine much of its surface, or stay put and sink a deep hole into its substance.

I was also very hungry. By the time I reached Ray's drive the sun had struck the far desert off to the west. The Jemez mountains lay pink and serene on the horizon, trembling as if seen through an old window. The house was bright inside, dissected by deep shadows, and quiet. Everyone was sleeping still. I had a bowl of cereal in the kitchen, then went along to the bedroom. I closed the door quietly, keeping the handle turned until I felt the little thud, then pulled the curtains shut and undressed.

Lisa was lying hunched over on her side. She rose up on a

little swell as I climbed into bed, then gently steadied out on the diminishing waves. She sighed once in her sleep, smacked her lips and was still.

FOURTEEN

Plain Sailing

I WOKE UP TO HEAR a light tapping, more of a scratching, on the door, and lifted my head. Lisa let out a short moan and turned away from me, catching one of my legs and pulling it with her, making me rock back and forth.

'Hello?' I said softly, propping myself up on my elbows and looking at the door. I thought maybe it was an insect, or the dog.

A funny voice answered, 'Helloo-oo.' The word coming out in three syllables, the greeting you would use for a child hiding under a table.

'Yes?'

The voice tittered. 'Natalie wants you,' it said, with an emphasis on the wants. It was Ray.

'What?'

'She's on line one.'

I thanked him and reached for the telephone on the counter beyond Lisa. As I put my weight on my knees they slipped away from beneath me and I fell on top of her. But she gave way under me too, heavily and easily, and we both came bouncing up again in slow motion.

'Sorry,' I said. I picked up the receiver. 'Hello?' There was no sound on the line. 'Hello?' I tried hanging up and listened again, but there was still no one there. 'What's going on?'

Lisa, who had rolled away so her thighs were beneath my ankles, mumbled: 'He said line one.'

'What does that mean?'

'Maybe it's a two-line phone or something.'

I pulled my ankles off her and had a better look and located the right button. A yellow light came on.

'Hello?'

She was there. 'I didn't mean to wake you,' she said.

'No, no, you didn't.'

I glanced at the clock. It was ten.

She asked me if I wanted to come and have lunch in her new house later on.

I had a shower and dressed. Meanwhile Lisa was watching a John Wayne movie on cable TV. I sat back on the bed and pulled on my boots and watched for a minute too. A stagecoach was driving along beneath one of those rugged, alternately sloping and stepping western cliffs. It was good to see it there. It looked like the sides of the canyon of the Rio Grande at Taos, where I had swum in the river and soaked in the hot spring. There it was, immortalized on the screen, the very land I was in.

Ray was in the kitchen, sitting at the table. 'Are you off?' he asked when I walked in.

'What?'

'You're off the phone, I take it?'

I nodded.

He picked up his cordless. 'Well, help yourself to some coffee. Barry, get him some coffee. And do you want some home fries? We're just having home fries and hot cakes. Does that sound good?' I thanked him and took the blue mug of coffee that Barry filled for me from the machine.

Ray dialled a number. While he waited for them to answer he said, 'And what about your girlfriend? Doesn't she want something? Barry's fixing it just now.'

Barry was at the counter grating potatoes into a white plastic bowl. Little slithers had stuck to the sides and a wet glistening heap was growing in the bottom. A black pan with a spill of oil was waiting on the cooker.

'Mm,' I said.

Barry shook his head. '*Real* home fries. No cheese. No onion. No nothin'. Just pure Idaho. This is how you make *home* fries.' A plastic pitcher of batter for the pancakes stood waiting beside the stove.

'I'll ask her,' I told Ray.

He raised his eyebrows at me, still listening to his telephone. Then he hung up, saying, 'I was trying Tommy Maccaione again. He's never in. We'll have to see him another time.'

I got back to the bedroom just as Lisa opened the door. Her hair was tousled and she smelled stale from lying in bed late. She had pulled on her green dress and her sandals. She glanced down at her hands. I stepped back to let her out.

'I'm on my way,' she said, raising her eyes to mine.

'You don't want breakfast? They're making some.'

She patted her belly. 'Still full.'

Last night we had eaten some tapas at the bar.

'Call me later?'

'Sure,' I said.

I walked out to her car.

She got in, started up and wound down the window. 'So where did you go?' She squinted at me.

'Go?'

'This morning.'

'Around town.'

'Was it nice?' She put on her dark glasses but her nose stayed screwed up like she was still squinting.

'Yes.' The engine was running softly. 'I like it here.'

She kept on looking at me. 'This house is weird. He's weird. They're all weird. I think you should leave.'

'What? I like it.'

She shook her head. 'Call me later.'

For an instant I saw her as an accomplished woman, a woman in her thirties with a good career who had just spent the night with her lover or husband and now was going off to attend to her business. She seemed a strong, good American woman. It's her looks, I told myself. It's hard not to read things into her when she has a face like that. But the truth was I was growing fond of her, even though I knew it was a bad idea to. She clearly wasn't interested in anything more than the most casual friendship, and at any moment she might suddenly decide to move on or hang out with someone else. But I found it difficult to keep reminding myself of that.

The fender winked at me as she drove away, the metallic blue paint of the car dazzling in the morning sunshine.

I ate pancakes and home fries with Ray and Barry. Jim was still in the house too. He came down the corridor from Ray's bedroom, tucking in his tank top and rubbing his eyes, and went straight to the coffee machine to pour himself a mug, into which he spooned four teaspoons of sugar. He settled himself at the table without a word and forked off five pancakes, which he drenched in maple syrup, and began eating his way silently through the stack.

Ray watched him for a while. 'Well, aren't you going to have any home fries? You know they're the best.'

Jim didn't respond.

'Would you like me to give you some?'

He kept on eating, scooping off big chunks of pancake with the side of his fork.

'Here.' Ray reached for the spoon in the home fries bowl and placed a chunk of the matted brown shreds on the side of his plate, delicately. Jim didn't look up, but kept on eating. Ray got another spoonful ready and this time, partly through lack of space, he delivered it on top of the remaining pancakes.

Jim slowed up. He allowed his empty fork to descend towards the table in slow-motion, with the menace of a cowboy who has just been insulted in a movie. For a moment I half expected him to pull a knife out. With a pang of remorse I thought of what Lisa had said. She was right. I should leave this house. But it was already too late.

Jim wasn't sure what to do next. He put his elbow on the table, nudging the plate away, then rested his forehead on the back of the hand with the fork. He pulled an old pack of Winstons out of his trouser pocket and rummaged inside it till he found a cigarette, stuck it in his mouth and discovered that he had no matches.

'Excuse me,' Ray said. 'Do you mind? Some people are still eating.'

He was referring to me. I was in the middle of my third and final pancake. I said, 'It doesn't bother me.'

'And you haven't finished either,' Ray went on.

'Yes I have,' Jim said. They were the first words he had uttered.

Ray guffawed. 'You think we don't know *your* appetite?'

'The original Mister Hollow Legs,' Barry said. He caught Ray's eye. 'Except for –' He broke into his hard laugh. 'That one's not hollow.'

Ray didn't laugh. He hissed, 'Don't be so silly.'

Barry let his laugh wind down.

'You mean you expect me to believe you're not going to eat that up?'

'I've finished,' Jim said again.

I felt it coming this time. It was as if the air changed, like the air before a storm: suddenly full of static, and too hot.

Ray started slow and worked himself up. 'You mean to say Barry cooks you a fabulous breakfast, all your favourite things just like you asked for, we put ourselves out every which way to make you happy and you haven't got the decency, the common decency, to eat up what you ask for? Is that what you're trying to tell me?'

Jim shook his head. 'God.'

'And now you expect me to run you home to your poor mother. Lord help her. I'm going to tell her about you. Yes I am. I'm going to tell her what kind of things her son does behind her back. I will too. How would you like that? How would you like that?'

By now he was rattling along, spewing little flecks of spittle. His face had turned the colour of a yam.

'And what do you think she'll say to that? When I tell her about her good little son and what her good little son does when he's out of the house? She'll be sorry they ever let you out of the State Pen. That's where you belong. That's –'

He paused and wiped a hand over his forehead, which was glistening. He lowered his eyes to the pancake bowl and seemed to study it for a moment, then let out a small, quavering moan. He put a hand to his chest and sat back in his chair. He kept on going back, however, and before I knew what was happening he had fallen to the floor. The table tipped for a moment as he fell, then dropped back onto its feet. A dribble of hot coffee seeped onto my thigh, and the pancake bowl slid into my lap. A number of things, forks and spoons, plates and cups, fell to the floor.

Barry was quick. He knelt beside Ray and felt his ribcage, then his forehead. He tugged at the neck of Ray's T-shirt. 'Just take it easy there. Take it easy. Everything's just fine.' Then the black dog appeared, wagging its tail and licking his face. Barry pulled her away. She squealed excitedly.

It was a moment before I realized that something serious had really happened. I didn't know what exactly, but at the very least Ray had fainted. I went to the telephone. 'Shall I call an ambulance?'

Barry told me to fetch some pills from the bathroom cabinet. By the time I got back Ray had come round. Barry held his head and fed him three pills, followed by a glass of water, which spilled all over his chin. Ray screwed up his face, spluttered and moaned, but seemed to swallow the dose. Barry laid his head down again.

'You just lie there and relax. Just close your eyes and relax. We'll get you to bed later on.'

Ray coughed. Then a small voice croaked from his lips, 'Call the doctor.'

'You want me to call the doctor?'

'He said to call him next time.' He let out another moan and closed his eyes. But you could see that his face was easing up already, turning a softer pink.

Jim was at the stove lighting his cigarette. He glanced at me as I moved away from the telephone, leaving it free, and shrugged at me. 'Want one?'

I shook my head.

'I don't know,' Barry said. 'Better not in the kitchen.'

Without a word Jim walked out onto the patio. I saw him shrug his shoulders again, take a drag, holding the cigarette shielded in his hand like a soldier in a movie, and kick the leg of one of Ray's chained chaises longues.

An ambulance came for Ray. They put him in a wheelchair.

'I won't be gone long,' he told me as they wheeled him through the living room. 'Just one night. Like last time. Right, guys?'

One of the ambulancemen said, 'Guess.'

The other said, 'Have to wait and see what the doctor says.'

'Just some tests,' Ray went on. 'That's all. Some more tests. Because of course we all know there's only one thing wrong with me. I've only got one problem, and it's called fat. I'm fat, that's all. I know what he'll do. He'll put me on fifteen hundred calories a day again.'

He looked down at the side of the chair. The men had bent low by each wheel, in preparation for lifting him up the step into the lobby with the fake waterfall. 'Ooph! You boys having a hard time there,' he observed. 'Nearly there. That's the hardest part. Plain sailing from now on in.'

Out on the path among the piñon bushes Ray gave Barry some instructions on locking up the house and feeding the dog. It seemed that Barry would be staying in his absence. 'And tell that rat I never want to see his tail round here again. All right?'

'Right.'

'And have yourselves a good time. Don't do anything I wouldn't do.' He tittered. 'Sianora.' He seemed in fine spirits.

The ambulancemen left as soon as they had Ray properly installed, and a little later I heard Barry's car drive out. He was giving Jim a lift home. I sat in my room for a while feeling troubled. I flipped through the channels on the cable TV, pausing at an old Robert Mitchum movie set in Mexico, but I wasn't in the mood. I lay back on the bed but found it made me think of Lisa. I got up again and went to the phone in the living room.

I tried Lisa. I wanted to talk to her. I had a plan and I wanted to see if she would join me. My idea was to go on a final trip round the state, passing through Las Vegas on the way, before deciding about whether or not to leave. I was hoping she would agree and we could go in her car. I tried her a few times and got no answer. Then I went to the kitchen and poured myself a cup of coffee from the machine, which got cold on the table before I remembered to drink it. In the meantime I stared out of the kitchen window, feeling unsettled. The mountains looked crystalline, severe in the late morning light.

I went back to the phone and tried her one last time. She was still out.

That afternoon Natalie and I planted five rows of spinach seeds in her back yard. I watered them with a hose, as well as the fibrous tomato plants that sprawled along the base of her garage wall. We ate a big lunch off chunky coloured plates and built a fire of piñon and cedar wood in the wood-stove. It got hot in the sitting room so we opened the front door, and eventually we sat out on the porch while Natalie told me about Santa Fe in winter, how quiet the town got and how fragrant with wood-smoke. All the adobe walls got frosted with snow, she said.

I called Lisa from a payphone after I left, and again at tea-time from home. I was beginning to wonder what had happened to her. Perhaps she had left town. She might have suddenly gone back east, I thought. She could have had some family disaster, or else suffered a powerful impulse to give up her drifting life in the west and go home. It wouldn't have surprised me. But most likely she was just cruising round town.

Which she was. I caught a glimpse of her that evening. It was at the stop sign on Galisteo and Paseo de Peralta. A Harley-Davidson with gleaming chopper bars pulled up. A native American with long black hair and a leather jacket was riding it, with a pretty young woman in jeans and short blonde hair jammed behind him. I thought I dimly recognized both of them, but it was a moment before I realized who they were. I saw her shoes first, the scuffed lace-ups with no laces. Then she leaned back against the rest, revealing the back of the driver's leather jacket, which was adorned with a mosaic of an eagle. It was Rocket in Pocket, with Lisa riding pillion.

I was about to wave and call out, but they roared off. I stopped and watched them go. He banked easily as he made the turn onto Paseo with the practised swoop of a seasoned rider. They looked good together, his long hair fluttering in the breeze, her face golden in the dusk. The motorbike hovered away into the hazy glow above the road.

When I got back I opened up Ray's woodstove and built a fire of old, dry pine logs from a basket. Outside, through the bushes, the sky was a brilliant, rich orange. The fire picked up and soon the ghosts of the flames were licking all over the ceiling and walls. I lay back on the carpet listening to the hisses and cracks of the pinewood and thought back over the day. A lot had happened. Ray had gone to hospital, a beautiful American writer had invited me to lunch, I had sat my first period of Zazen, and Lisa had apparently moved on. I could see her now tearing over the gleaming tarmac into the sunset. I imagined her roaring all the way to Seattle, to Portland, to San Francisco. I could see her high up above the ocean on the Golden Gate Bridge, and the ocean stretching out to the west, always beyond her.

FIFTEEN

The Tallest Mountain on Earth

I MADE MY TRIP without Lisa. A friend of Natalie's had a heavy old truck rusting in their yard, which they offered to let me run for a week. It was a Bronco Mark I, a great hunk of Ford iron with eight thirsty, noisy cylinders, and wheels designed for tackling any terrain. I set out to put its versatility to use.

My first leg was out west, to the Jemez mountains. I had looked at them long enough. From across the plain, in Santa Fe, they formed a ridge of strange undulating curves and sharp little peaks standing out against the evening sky, or jagged like an ice-floe in the moonlight, with the lights of Los Alamos clustered beneath them. I wanted to get into them now, find out what they were really like. The Bronco gurgled across the flat land towards them, slowly gathering momentum, until we were hurtling along at a perilous fifty-five.

I had meant to leave early. My plan was to stop at the Spence Springs, some hot springs in the mountains that had been popular in the '60s. A friend had given me approximate directions, and I thought I would begin my excursion with a dip in the hot water, and proceed feeling purified towards some wayside motel. But I didn't finally get away till the middle of the afternoon. When I left, Santa Fe was basking in September sunshine, hot and still and sparkling. But as I drove west the weather changed, and the Jemez mountains vanished behind a bank of lead clouds on the horizon.

The journey to the springs was supposed to take an hour. I rolled into the town of Los Alamos, bedded up against the flank of the mountains, in fifty minutes. By then the afternoon had got so dark I had to use the headlights. An uneasiness crept up on me. The town was eerie, draped in a thin fog coming off the hills, with its road signs covered with meaningless code-numbers and every few blocks a security gate into some secret laboratory. The rows of suburban houses built along the edge of the canyon that ran through the town seemed temporary, disposable. They didn't seem like homes. There was an airstrip full of executive aircraft for rushing the scientists in and out. It was strange to have driven suddenly out of the sunny desert into this dark town created specially for the Manhattan Project, which had developed the most powerful destructive devices ever known.

Things got stranger still when I pulled out of the town and started climbing into the mountains. The afternoon darkened abruptly, and the sky turned the colour of a restless Hebridean sea. A storm was obviously brewing, and it seemed only a matter of time before it broke. But it never came. Instead it got so cold inside the Bronco I had to turn on the heater and close the windows. I found myself driving up a long steep hill into thick forest when suddenly a light drumming began on the cab roof. It quickly became a deafening roar, while the road ahead turned silver-white. At first I thought it was a tremendous downpour. But it wasn't: I was caught in the middle of a hailstorm.

I slowed right down, crawled along under the pelting with the lights on high beam. They picked out a white bamboo curtain, which hung always just in front of me. Then the hail stopped as abruptly as it had started, leaving in its wake a listless, quiet fall of unseasonal snowflakes. I turned the heating fan to maximum and wondered how high up I was.

˙Meanwhile the Bronco wasn't doing well in the cold. Every few moments it would splutter and threaten to stall, then suddenly the automatic choke would kick in and I would find myself struggling to rein it in. The mix of snow and hail and cold had left a film of slush on the road, and my frantic attacks on the brakes sent the truck into slow, graceful skids towards either ditch, like an elephant on ice. It wasn't that big a truck, but it handled like it was made of wrought iron.

I was getting worried now. I had been driving well over an hour and a half and I was still climbing into the hills. I was supposed to have reached the Spence Springs some time ago. And I was running low on gas. I had been waiting for the reserve fuel light to come on, until I realized that there wasn't one. The needle was resting against the pin already. And the Jemez were turning out to be a wild, empty range. It was like the landscape of a Russian fairy-tale, or the famous Canadian ghost story about the Wendigo monster: mile after mile of uninhabited forest.

I passed a sign saying: 'Jemez Springs 38'. Jemez Springs was a town a few miles beyond the hot springs, which meant I still had at least thirty miles to go. I picked up the map and held it over the steering wheel as I drove, wondering if there would be a gas station before then. There was nowhere marked. Thirty-eight miles of emptiness. An hour of nothing, no humans, no houses, just ancient forest. And there were cougars in the Jemez. These mountains were one of their last stalks. I understood suddenly the eighteenth-century fear of nature, of, say, the highlands of Scotland, as a desert, a bad place, a place to avoid, or to civilize.

Finally the snow eased up and the road stopped climbing. I came out of the forest onto a huge plain, a great saucer in the mountains. Far away, all around it, dark mountains rose up, closing it in. It was the old crater of a giant volcano that had blown up a million years ago, and which had once been the highest mountain on earth, two miles taller than Everest. All that remained was its base, which was the entire hundred miles of the Jemez range, with the crater in the middle, now covered with lush tall grass like a buffalo plain, and in the weak afternoon light beneath a high overcast sky the grassland was soft and pale, a yellow cloud reaching to the black hills on the far side.

The road straightened out and I drove fast. I knew that the faster

I drove the sooner I would run out of fuel, but I was scared of arriving at a gas station after it closed. It seemed likely that out here if I did happen to find one it would close at around five or six at the latest.

It wasn't long till I saw lights ahead, just two points in the darkness. They rolled closer from bend to bend, until I could see a junction, a house, and a blue neon sign. Then I could read the sign. It said 'High Sierra Motel'. Another sign appeared beyond it, saying, 'Gas Up In Back,' in red neon. There was a store too, and a restaurant. I gunned the truck still harder, imagining the store and gas pumps being just about to close, the owner about to lock up and drive off to a cabin up in the woods. But I had no need to hurry. The pumps were still lit up when I pulled in.

I filled up. It was cold out, and the air was thin. I discovered I had a headache, and mixed in with it was that light-headed feeling of high altitude. Somehow the sensation seemed to match the buildings, which were wooden and flimsy.

I opened the door into the store to pay for the petrol. Right in front of me, on top of a rack of shelves, stood a cougar. I noticed the glare of its glass case, and the dusty bulk within, before I realized what it was: a heavy, sleek animal the size of a lion, spotted, with a long cheetah tail, a real mountain lion, the kind the Homeric shepherds had to fight off. They had died out long ago in Europe, but they still had them here. This was still a young land, a new land, a frontier. Pinned to the case was a photograph of a man with a gun over his elbow, and the cougar strung up beside him by its front paws. The animal was taller than him.

Two cars were already parked in the lot by the hot springs, a Nissan pick-up and a tiny Honda with a high-power CB antenna on its roof. I switched off the engine, turned off the lights. In the dark the great valley walls had become ghostly black presences like cliffs of ice in an Arctic night. On the far side, above a high crest, there was a yellow smudge in the sky where the moon would rise. The sound of a rushing stream filled the night.

I found a path down to the torrent and crossed over on a log. A trail led up through the trees. As I climbed, it became muddier and the air turned dank and warm. The path weaved between big boulders. I wasn't exactly sure what I was looking for – a steaming stream, a pool like the one near Taos, a waterfall? – but I guessed I was getting close. Then suddenly I saw it below me, behind a big boulder: a wide pool, dammed up with a row of rocks. Two very white men were sitting in the water. Moonlit steam trailed up from their white arms into the sky. Beyond them, the valley side fell away, and there was a view over the whole wide canyon, with a half moon hanging just above the far hills.

'Hi,' one of the men called. 'It's around a hundred and ten. A little hotter than usual.'

I figured there was nothing for it but to undress and climb in.

'You can get in over there,' the same man advised. 'But watch out for that big kinda slippy rock under the water.' He was the older of the two, sitting on a stone with his ankles dangling in the pool, his arms draped on his thighs. He had a short black beard and a thick bush of pubic hair, an oddly pale-looking penis resting in it.

'That's a good perch over there,' he went on.

After I settled in he said, 'Well, I'm Jim. And this here's Donald.'

'Hi,' said the other man, who looked in his twenties, and had wavy fair hair and a pair of porthole glasses. He spoke very softly. We all sat in silence for a while, feeling self-conscious.

Jim explained about the geology of the hot springs, how pressure forced the hot water up from a stratum above a lava bed. As he talked I realized I was not only feeling inhibited but nervous: here I was sitting naked with two strange men, also naked, as night fell in the wilds of America. If they were perverts or murderers or both they were now entirely free of all restraints. They could do whatever they liked to me. I could scream, even fire off a gun if I had one, and there would be no one to hear for miles around. Only once that night, later, did lights suddenly start playing on the rocks as a car wound up the canyon.

I decided it was too late to do anything now, so I might as well enjoy it, and lay back in the hot water looking up at the tall thick pine trees and the stars caught on their high twigs, and saw a shooting star, then a satellite.

'That one's on polar orbit,' Jim told me. 'You don't see too many of them.'

I put my head under water and opened my eyes. I could see my legs, two blurred white logs in the blue light. The heat hurt my eyes. I spent at least as long sitting out of the water cooling off, as I did in it. You sat in the freezing, clear night watching the water evaporate from your arms. In under a minute it left your skin feeling tight and springy. When you began to feel the cold you slipped back in to heat up again.

Jim told me he ran a computer system in Los Alamos. When I asked he said it had nothing to do with bombs. He had spent a year unemployed out in Boston and came west three years ago. 'Never again,' he said. 'It nearly did me in, not working.'

I felt a twinge of guilt: I had given up my regular job. Here I was chasing some unidentifiable phantom in New Mexico, instead of buckling down back home. Jim shifted the talk to handguns and rifles, and a recent self-defence case in which a young office-worker had shot a woman in a parking lot whom he believed to be about to draw a gun on him. Jim said he always carried a gun.

Just then a warble rang out in the night.

'Damn,' Jim exclaimed. It was his car alarm. We all sat listening to it for a minute. It was a strange, incongruous sound out in the wilderness, yet somehow comforting. Then it stopped.

'Gosh darn,' he said. 'I just hope it was the wind. It could rock the CB antenna, I guess.' He picked up the gun talk where he had left off.

I was only half listening. I was wondering how long I would stay, where I would try to get to tonight. My thoughts kept drifting around to Lisa. I was curious to know when she had met Rocket in Pocket, if she had been seeing him for some time. I knew it made no difference anyway, and reflected that someone who stepped into your life so easily was likely to step out of it equally readily, but somehow the hot water and the moonlight and the canyon made me think of her. It would have been good to be here with her.

I realized I had had enough of the place, and climbed back to my clothes to look at the time. My gear was in a heap, and I reached under the trousers and shirt to where I thought I had left my jacket. It wasn't there. I searched the surrounding rocks. There was no sign of it. I tried to remember if I had left it somewhere else after all, but I was sure I had used it as a base to pile the rest of my clothes on. I started looking further afield, and found the jacket on a different rock all by itself a few feet below, where I was quite sure I hadn't left it.

I checked the time: six-thirty. It was fully dark now, and I figured it was time to leave. Jim came lumbering out to his clothes, Donald following. 'You had enough?' I asked.

'Got to get back. Night shift.'

It made me uneasy that they were both leaving now too, at the same time as me. For some reason I vaguely associated them with the odd movement of my jacket, though they could hardly have had anything to do with it, since they had been sitting in the pool with me the entire time. But I didn't mention it. They dressed in silence. Suddenly everything felt sinister, nothing was dependable.

Then Donald announced: 'I can't find my keys.' He checked his pockets twice, and we all groped among the rocks in the dark. At that point I told them about my jacket.

'Damn,' Jim said. 'I guess some robber stole up on us. You lost anything?'

I hadn't thought to look: it had seemed so improbable that there would be a thief up here. My wallet was still in my trousers.

We failed to turn up Donald's keys, and headed downhill, hoping he had left them in his truck. Back at the parking lot Donald immediately went to his Nissan pick-up and found it locked up as he had left it, and no sign of his keys. Jim opened his little Honda, saw something on the front seat and reached in.

'Well I'll . . .' he exclaimed. On his seat were a set of keys, not his own. They turned out to be Donald's.

'Darn,' Jim said. 'Someone's been playing tricks on us.' It was certainly strange. Someone had apparently moved my jacket from under my clothes to a nearby rock, and then been through Donald's gear, found his keys – and all while we were a few feet away in the hot water – then somehow opened up Jim's car and left the keys inside it.

Jim reached into the back of his Honda and pulled up the seat. He emerged holding a pair of elaborate binoculars, with extended lenses and a variety of dials. He lifted them to his eyes and scanned the valley sides for a minute, then lowered them and confided to me: 'Infra red. I think I've got him. See that big old tree over there, kinda white? He's behind it.'

He reached into his knapsack and took out a pistol. ''Fore I go get him, let's see who's lost what.'

I checked my bags and pockets again. I took out my wallet and opened it up and found to my surprise that all the money in it, only a few dollars, had gone. Fortunately I had most of my cash in the glove box of the Bronco. I checked and it was still there. Donald had lost some money too.

I tried to dissuade Jim from chasing the thief, but he was adamant, and seemed to know what he was about. With his binoculars in one hand and the pistol in the other he disappeared into the woods. While he was gone Donald silently made his way back to his truck, now that his keys had been recovered, and started up the engine. The lights came on and the truck rumbled slowly forwards, hissing and crunching as the wheels turned on the ground. He positioned it so the headlights flared on the trees where Jim was conducting his operations.

I thought I heard a distant moan, but I wasn't sure. I stood waiting, suddenly feeling cold. Eventually Donald got out of his truck, leaving the engine running and the lights on. We heard nothing more, no gun shots or shouts, only the distant rushing of the stream. After a while we both climbed into his truck and switched on the heater. I was restless and uneasy and would have liked to have left, but felt an obligation to wait and see how Jim fared.

Eventually he came jogging back into the parking lot and rapped on the truck window. He was rubbing his eyes with the heel of the hand that held the pistol.

'Must've seen me coming.' His breaths were rasping in and out through his thick beard. 'What the hell were you doing giving him a chance like that? And you darn near blinded me. These are night-vision tubes.'

Donald apologized and nervously switched off his headlights, as if it might make a difference now. Jim screwed his eyes tight, then blinked at us, and started going through lengthy post-mortems both of what he had done in the woods, and of the crime itself. But as we already knew, his manoeuvrings had come to nothing, and now all I wanted to do was get away. So far this hadn't been an auspicious start to my trip around the state.

I climbed out of the warm truck, said goodbye to them, and opened up the Bronco. Jim followed me over to his Honda, which was parked beside it.

'I'm gonna have to get myself a darn check-up,' he said. 'You can fry your eyes with these things. What a bozo. Some people don't know anything. Where you headed anyway?'

'South,' I told him.

'Be sure and remember to take off that jacket.' He let out a forced, lonely laugh. 'It's hot down there.'

I laughed back. I sensed that he wanted some acknowledgement of his heroics and was reluctant to be alone just now. It crossed my mind that he had only pulled out his equipment in the hope of winning the friendship of two strangers, whose company he had fallen into. He seemed just the kind of lonely technophile who belonged in a place like Los Alamos. I felt both sorry and uneasy, and was relieved when a moment's lull opened in his talk, and I managed to take my leave.

It was good to get on the road again. I had a full tank of petrol, a road that pointed south, and far ahead something to aim for, a faint orange tinge in the sky that I knew to be the lights of Albuquerque. I let the momentum build from bend to bend as I soared down the canyon, through the town of Jemez Springs, through San Ysidro, and back onto the plain, working my way south and east. By the time the glow of Albuquerque engulfed me it was quarter to eight, and I was in no mood to stop.

SIXTEEN

Hot Springs

I FLEW THROUGH ALBUQUERQUE, joining the pack of traffic on I–25 for the fifteen-mile stretch of city exits, then filing out south onto the dark desert on the far side of town. Having had a look at the Jemez my plan now was to get into the Black mountains further south. I had spotted an all-weather dirt track on my map, called County 52, which I hoped would carry me back in a big loop through the mountains to Albuquerque, from where I would finally go east to Las Vegas, New Mexico, and see if I could find the Flying Father.

It was good to be on a plain again. It was warm out. I opened the window and rested my elbow on the sill, feeling the dusty desert air blast the side of my face. Now and then a green sign for an exit crept towards me: Isleta, Los Lunas, Polvadera, Socorro. I thought of turning off and stopping for the night, but I wanted to hold out till I got to the town of Truth or Consequences. The dirt track I intended to explore set out from there, and I hoped to get an early start on it. But also I was intrigued by the town's name.

A sign on the edge of Albuquerque had listed 'T or C' as one hundred and forty-six miles away. I managed to coax the Bronco up to fifty-eight miles an hour and exactly two and a half hours later I let my foot off the accelerator and the truck spluttered and farted onto a slip road off the highway. A bridge led back across the road – on which just then, as I crossed over, I couldn't see a single head or tail light – then onto a long strip of trailer parks, drive-in movie theatres and motels. The strip got denser, the businesses packed closer together, and a few cars passed me going the other way. I had to stop at a traffic light. Then the stores thinned out again. I passed one more trailer park called the Elephant Park – after Elephant Butte, a nearby mountain and lake – and I was back on the desert. I had passed right through town.

I turned round and headed back.

I selected a motel called the Hot Springs. It seemed appropriate. Puddles lying here and there on the muddy yard in front caught a red gleam from a street lamp. I picked my way among them towards the main door. The air was curiously clammy, something like the air in a Turkish bath in the morning before all the steamers have been switched on. I caught a whiff of sulphur on the breeze.

I opened the door into a long empty hallway, where the smell of sulphur was stronger. A row of sunbeds stood along the wall, and three white plastic table and chair sets further down waited for occupants. It was evidently an unusual motel: it provided relaxation areas for its guests, and had a reception hall rather than an office.

There was no bell on the desk. All the lights were on. I coughed out loud, feeling a little shy. Then I called out, 'Hello?'

No one came. I called again, then scrutinized a photograph hanging on the wall, entitled 'Hot Springs High, Class of 1954'. Rows of small faces grinned at the camera from under dark heads of hair. One beautiful young woman on the end of a row pouted without trace of a smile, her hair a mess. She looked like a rebel. I wondered what had happened to her since, if she still lived here or had become a hippie in San Francisco or a junkie in New York. Or she might have become a tired housewife in one of the trailer parks, working part-time as a waitress in a local diner.

A door scraped open somewhere in the interior of the building and footsteps approached. A dark figure appeared in a frosted glass door. An old man in a lumberjack shirt shuffled out.

'Good evening, sir,' he said, installing himself on a stool with his hands up on the counter. 'What may we do for you?' He had pale, wrinkled hands, the hands of a pickler.

179

I told him I wanted a room.

'Just a room? No bath?' He raised his bushy white eyebrows and stared at me with a pair of sparkling eyes. He had more than a passing resemblance to Albert Einstein.

'Bath?'

'Yes, sir, a bath. We have hot sulphur baths here, sir, and many of our guests come for the waters. We're built right on top of a hot lake, sir. Floating on it, you might say.'

I asked him if the site for the motel had been chosen for that reason.

'In a manner. The whole town's here for the waters. There's hot lakes everywhere. Under the A and P, under the Yucca Drive-in, under the Elephant Park. But we have a constant temperature here. Most folks are a hundred and twenty one week, a hundred the next.'

'What are you?' I asked.

'One hundred and fifteen degrees, year in, year out.' He shook his head. 'Wouldn't want it any hotter than that.'

I asked whether the high school of the photograph was named after these same sulphur springs.

'The whole town was named after them.'

I didn't understand.

'Used to be the town of Hot Springs, sir, and there are some of us who wish it still was.'

'The town changed its name to Truth or Consequences?'

He nodded. 'Our last mayor was a big fan of the TV show. You'll know the show. He took them up on their search for a town that would change its name and call itself after them. So there you are. And in the opinion of some of us there was nothing wrong with the name we had. Still, we all get used to change sooner or later. Have to.'

I agreed. 'It's certainly an unusual name,' I added.

He mumbled something I didn't catch, then said, 'So. Just a room. Well, why not take a bath in the morning? Let me know

180

what time and I'll draw it for you. Piping hot, waiting first thing.'
I smiled.

'Sounds good, huh? All right, then.' He spoke broadly, with
reserved triumph. 'What time, then?'

We settled it at eight the next morning.

The room was nothing special. After dumping my bag on the
bed and opening it up and forgetting what I had planned to take
out, I left and climbed into the Bronco, which was waiting immediately outside the room, like a cowboy's horse outside the bunkhouse, and drove off up the road to look for a late supper.

The Silver Dollar Diner was still open. I nudged the Bronco up
against the fence in the parking lot. Inside flashing lights hung
along the top of the wall and lengths of tinsel had been taped here
and there, to the till, on the edge of the counter, along the lintel
of a doorway, for some recent anniversary. On a shelf high up, a
long traffic jam of toy cars made its way right the way round the
room, up above the booths of fake black leather. There were only
two other customers, a young man and an older man, both wearing
white shirts and ties and sitting at the same table.

The waitress quietly, smilingly led me to the table next to theirs.
I ordered a chicken burrito and a Miller High Life and began to
listen in on their conversation.

'One more to go, Dale. That's all,' the younger man was saying.
'You realize you shift that one, that *one*, and you're making Vegas?
You realize that, Dale?'

The older man fingered his glass of beer, leaning back in his seat,
and said, 'Yeah, well.'

At first I had put them down as Mormons because of their dress,
but now I wasn't so sure. They were drinking beer for one thing.
I couldn't remember, but it seemed likely Mormons were teetotal.

The younger man shook his head. 'Heck, Dale, it's been one hell
of a week. It sure has.' He was beaming. 'You reckon I helped?
Helped things along?'

The older man laughed, a chesty, loose, cough-like laugh. 'Well, sure you did, Junior. You keep it up and you'll be going to Vegas too one day. Sure you will.'

It seemed a mannered conversation, somehow anachronistic. I was curious to know what that one thing they had left was, and to know what they did. They clearly both had some reason to feel pleased with themselves. They fell silent, drinking from their glasses of beer. Junior let out an exaggerated sigh of appreciation as he put his glass down. 'Sure tastes good at the end of the day, don't it?'

My food arrived. I ate slowly, listening to their intermittent chatter. At one point Junior had a good laugh about some woman Dale had insisted on visiting alone. 'Sure, I understand,' he said a few times, letting out a hard, deliberate laugh. He had a handsome face, neat razored hair, and I imagined I heard a hint of a jealous edge in his laughter, somewhere in with all the admiration for his superior.

Dale shook his head, trying not to smile. He wore steel-frame glasses and they flashed as he moved his face. 'Tricky move, tricky move. Had to come up on her gentle, kind of.'

This provoked more exaggerated laughter from the other side of the table. 'You got there too. Bingo!'

Dale sat back, eyeing his fresh glass of beer. 'Just about. Just about got there. Took my time. There's a lesson for you, Junior. Take your time. They'll sign on that line if you'll just take your time.'

I got it then. They were salesmen. They no doubt had certain quotas and if they reached them they won bonuses such as that trip to Las Vegas. I relaxed and found a smile rising to my lips. I felt as if I was sitting with friends now.

As I was finishing my plate I heard the young man say, 'Care to join us?' I didn't take it in and carried on eating, daydreaming simultaneously about my drive the next day. I was imagining meeting a cougar in the Black mountains.

'Care to join us for a drink?' he repeated.

I looked up. The young man was smiling at me. I faltered for a moment, then accepted. He slid along the bench to make room for me. We all shook hands. Dale insisted on buying me another Miller High Life, together with a round of José Cuervo Gold for us all. The waitress apologized, explaining they didn't have a liquor licence, and went to fetch my beer.

I asked if they lived in New Mexico.

'Nope. We're just out for one week. From Kansas City. Come down here once a year.'

Dale asked me to guess what they were doing in the state.

'Selling insurance?' I tried.

He raised his eyebrows and let out a long sigh, at the end of which he shook his head. 'Long ways off. Not even close.'

'No,' Junior agreed. 'Not even close.'

'Go on, you tell him,' Dale said.

'All right'. Junior pulled himself up in his seat. 'Corbies. You ever heard of Corbies?'

I indicated that I hadn't.

'Corby vacuum cleaners. Best domestic vacuum cleaner your money can buy. You got carpets, curtains, bedspreads, all your furniture – tell the truth, there isn't a stick or a stitch of anything in the whole damn house you can't steam, clean, polish or transform with a Corby. Once you've had one in your house a day, that's it. You'll never look back.'

He was obviously falling into his sales spiel. He just as obviously realized this might be an inappropriate time for it, but was apparently powerless to stop himself, or perhaps decided he would take this opportunity to show off in front of his boss. He went on for a while, glancing at Dale now and then, who stared at the table giving nothing away. I smiled at first, looking Junior in the eye, then felt embarrassed as it continued, and didn't know where to look. He came to the end, his eyes shining, and said, 'Well, what do you say?'

'If I had a house I'd buy one. But I'm a vagrant.'

Junior roared with laughter, assuming this must be some joke. Dale smiled at him, then turned to ask where I was from.

'England.'

'An out-of-stater too. Where are you staying?'

'At the Hot Springs Motel.'

'The old hothouse. Don't open the window whatever you do.' He grinned.

'Why not?'

He shook his head. 'You didn't notice? Maybe the wind was blowing the wrong way.'

'The sulphur?'

'Not too pleasant first thing in the morning.' He grimaced.

'I'm having a bath in it tomorrow,' I told him.

'You bought, eh?'

'What?'

'He made a sale. Old Johnson. Good for him.' He let out a wheezing laugh, as if having a good laugh about some absent fool, namely me, who had been squarely duped.

I shrugged. We took long pulls on our beers.

I asked Dale about life on the road, how many weeks he did in a year.

'As many weeks as there are in a year,' he answered. 'Yes, sir, I'm one of the originals. Never stop. Know the motels of the south-west better than anyone by now, I guess. They know me too. Number of them are clients, as a matter of fact.' He chuckled.

I was amazed. I didn't think people still lived like this in the age of telecommunications and mail order.

'Not many of you left, I suppose,' I said.

He let out a splutter of laughing disagreement. 'Come up to Vegas and see. I'll bet there's ten road sales conventions in town that week. And that's the tip of the iceberg, don't forget.'

Junior, perhaps feeling a little superstitious on his boss's behalf, said, 'Yup, we'll get Vegas in the bag tomorrow. We sure will.'

On the way out Dale urged me to buy a jar of hot sauce from

a little pyramid by the cash register. I acquiesced, just to please him, feeling certain I would never touch the jar.

'Best sauce there is,' he told me. 'Be careful.'

It had a purple label, not exactly homemade, but low-budget-looking, and was called, 'Religious Experience Hot Sauce. The Wrath!!!'

'You get yourself some nice chips and try that tomorrow out on County 52. You'll have a swell day, I guarantee it.' He was obviously pleased with himself at having capped off a good day with this last little sale on someone else's behalf, feeling his skill to be just about uncontainable.

I thanked him for the tip and climbed into the Bronco. Junior came over to the window to shake my hand. I wound down the glass and obliged. Then I put the jar in the glove box and turned the key. The engine chortled, shook itself and roared awake. Dale and Junior opened up a white sedan with dark red seats and settled themselves with a final wave. Gently I eased the gear stick over the brush into reverse. The car jolted and I let off the brake, gurgling backwards into the night.

The ten bathtubs were in a tiled hall at the end of the reception area, each in its own cubicle. High above, windows made of glass blocks let in a filtered white light. A thin cloud of steam lifted up from one of the cubicles, and I could hear water thundering out of a tap.

The old man, who was apparently called Johnson, wasn't around. I pushed open the lightweight door. Steaming water roared into the tub, landing in a milkshake of bubbles. The water had a faint green tinge. The bath was filling fast and there was no handle on the tap, just a brass nut too small to turn with the bare hand.

I wondered if I should try to find Old Johnson and warn him of the impending flood, when he came shuffling down the hallway with a yellow spanner in his hand. He greeted me and went straight in and turned off the tap.

'And when you get out you wrap yourself up in these,' he said, handing me a heavy bundle of towels. 'Then go lie on that bed.' He pointed to the nearest in a row of couches. 'I'll call you when your time's up. You just lay in that tub till then. You'll hear me rapping on your door.'

I closed the door and stripped off, looking at the wisps of steam coming off the tinted water. Oddly, they bore no odour of sulphur. It was a deep tub. I sat on the edge a long time before I swung the first leg over. Just as I had feared, the water was ferocious, so hot that it seemed to be not only hot but also acidic, as if *pétillant* with some astringent mineral. I drew my foot out pink and throbbing, and couldn't imagine how I was going to get in.

I waited, then tried the foot again. Gradually, joint by joint, I managed to ease both legs in, and finally underwent the scalding of the nether parts, in a series of dips, until I could actually sit in the tub. By then my face was already dripping sweat. It plopped from my chin into the water. My hair was wet with sweat too, and I felt lightheaded. I was also dizzy, as if I might pass out if I tried to stay upright. Without thinking about it, I lay back in the water.

The giddiness increased. I turned my head from side to side in hope of clearing it, suffered a brief flash of nausea, and the next thing I knew the whole room was reeling upwards like a ride at the fair and I was rolling off, falling into darkness.

When I came to Old Johnson was standing in the cubicle. For some reason I wasn't surprised to see him there. Nor did it surprise me to see him bending over the end of the tub with his sleeve rolled up and his arm in the water. He pulled out the plug, mumbled, 'You ain't supposed to fall asleep,' and shuffled out, leaving the door open.

I felt the waterline like a wire retreating down my body, letting in the cool air. I heard the plug-hole gurgling away between my ankles, and lay there in the still-hot tub till I could move again.

Johnson was waiting for me. He obviously didn't take kindly to people passing out in his baths. Frowning, without a word of solace, he told me to go lay down and he would wrap me up himself. His tone suggested that I couldn't be trusted to do it myself. I pulled a towel round my waist and went along with his orders, moving through a thoughtless heat haze, as he had me lie down on the couch and threw several towels on top of me, tucking them in tightly, creating a heat-wrap for me. When I was as snug as a caterpillar in its cocoon, he left the room.

I was still only partially conscious, but it was enough to know that I wasn't going to be able to stay like that for long. Already my face was prickling with fresh sweat, and I had a thirst so intense I felt it behind my throat, in a place no drink would ever reach. The hidden reserves of fluid in my body had drained away, and I felt like I had 'flu. The last thing I needed was to be trapped in a tight airless womb.

I tried to endure it for a few minutes, thinking of how I had conquered the pain in my leg at the Zen Center, endeavouring to focus on my breathing and allow that to carry me through. But it didn't work, and soon enough I pulled out first one arm, then the other. I stayed like that for a while, then folded the towel down just below my chest. Slowly I worked it lower and lower. First my diaphragm felt like it desperately needed to be in the open air, then my belly needed it, then my lower abdomen and finally my legs too. With a great relief I tore off all the towels, damp and hot with sweat, and dropped them on the floor, and lay naked and comfortable at last, knowing Old Johnson might come back and find me like that, but not caring.

The heat slowly escaped from my skin, like water evaporating. The fog in my head gradually cleared, as if blown on by a fresh wind, and finally I was clear-headed enough to make my way to the shower booth at the end of the room. I slumped onto the tiles and pulled down the handle. A deluge of icy water fell on top of me. I raised my face to it gratefully.

After a rub-down with a towel I began to feel better. I was aware of a deep glow spreading through my body. I dressed, my clothes feeling smooth and good against my freshened skin, and let myself out into the morning in a state of vibrant health, ready to hunt up a big breakfast and take on any mountain track, and glad that I had made up for the disappointing hot springs in the Jemez mountains.

When I paid, Johnson made no reference to the bath. I noticed that he didn't charge me for it either. I pointed this out to him.

He shrugged. 'We like our guests to be happy so they'll come again.'

I told him I was happy, I felt great.

'Forget about it,' he said.

I thought of Dale and wondered what he would have made of that, and thanked him.

'Any time,' he murmured, looking down at the papers on the counter.

'It's certainly the hottest water I've ever been in,' I added, hoping this would please him.

He didn't look up but his eyebrows twitched and I thought I could see the beginnings of a smile on his lips. 'Like I said, any time,' he repeated.

SEVENTEEN

Dialogue with an Alien

THE FIRST TOWN I hit was Chloride. It wasn't much of a town, just five or six derelict houses like a ghost town in a Clint Eastwood movie. The chloride they mined here had clearly run out some time ago, or else the market had dropped. It was on the edge of the plain, in the foothills of the Black mountains. Behind me, far away now, I could just make out the long dry crest that ran the far side of Truth or Consequences, known as Elephant Butte. Ahead were big green hills, smooth mountainsides dotted with cattle and patched with gulleys of black woodland.

The road forded a pair of shallow brown rivers, rolled through Winston, another deserted mining town, and carried me into the square of Cuchillo, surrounded by small white wooden houses. This was the last town before I really hit the mountains, and consisted of some twenty homes, mostly dilapidated, and a handful of scrawny mesquite trees.

I stopped at the one store, an old wooden building with a heavy sagging porch and a sign up above saying, 'Cuchillo General Store'. I pushed through a swing saloon door into a high room crammed with all kinds of goods. There were old 1950s refrigerated Coca-Cola vending machines, stacks of tinned food, a flip-top freezer full of ice cream; up on the shelves, guns, cases of bullets, reels of fishing line; hanging on the walls, snowshoes, two tennis rackets and a string bag of balls; and on the floor, shovels, pitchforks, Wellington boots. It was truly a general store. Beyond the front room a narrow doorway took you into a pool hall with two old tables and a whole gallery of deer and moose heads up on the walls. Old billiard lights hung over the tables, and two spinning cue racks stood in a far corner. I walked quietly around the room, wondering where the shop assistants were, giving the cue racks a nudge as I passed. They clicked satisfyingly round on their spindles, showing me their array of arms.

Through another doorway I discovered a long thin bar with windows so dusty you couldn't see anything through them. Seated behind the bar, watching a scratchy portable television on the end of the counter, was a woman with long blonde hair. She picked up a cigarette wedged in an ashtray as I walked in, took a long draw, and without turning to look at me, said, 'What can I get you?' The words came out wreathed in smoke.

The question took me by surprise. I was shocked at finding her here, so settled, so calm.

'I'll take a Bud,' I said, before I had even decided that I wanted a drink.

She took another pull on her cigarette. 'No Bud. Dos Equis, Corona, Sol.' She didn't look at me. She was engrossed in some soap I didn't recognize.

'Dos Equis, thanks.'

Without shifting from her perch on a stool, without even taking down the foot that was propped up on the bar, she reached down, clicked open a cold-cupboard by feel, took out the drink, selecting the right beer bottle the same way, flipped off the top on an opener under the bar and slid it over to me, then reached back down to clunk the door shut again, and all without taking her eyes off the TV.

'Glass?'

'What?'

'You want a glass for your beer?'

'No, thanks.'

She lifted her cigarette again. 'You need anything else, you let me know.'

I sat on a stool watching the show with her in silence. A couple were having an intense debate about another woman called Debbie. It seemed one of them knew something the other one didn't, and they weren't letting on.

I wandered back into the games room with my bottle, to study a few deer heads. There were some big heads there, some splendid antlers. The glassy eyes stared in perplexed innocence at the billiard lights. Over in the corner a great black bear's face had burst through the wall, also looking surprised and baffled by the room he found himself in. On a small table, beside a Jack Daniels ashtray, lay a pile of copies of a pamphlet called 'A Hunter's Memoirs'.

I picked one up. It was a cheaply printed book, full of typos, written by a local farmer. He declared at the start that he wasn't much of a story-teller, which enticed me to read on, but unfortunately he was right. Each chapter had an exciting title like 'In Search of the Great Black Bear', or 'The Day We Finally Found the Killer Cougar', but they were all confusingly similar – repetitive accounts of how his dogs would chase the quarry up and down a valley and eventually 'get it treed'. This meant driving the terrified beast up into a tree, where the farmer could easily pick it off with his rifle. It didn't reveal whether the heads in this very room were the author's trophies, or some rival's.

Then I remembered the hot sauce Dale had persuaded me to buy the night before. I needed a bag of chips to go with it, and found some in the store. Just as I went into the bar to pay for them the ads started on the TV. The lady turned to me. I saw she was wearing a pink lipstick to match her pink sweatshirt. Long grey roots were growing in the middle of her blonde hair-do. She looked at my bag of chips on the bar, glanced at me from behind a pair of pink-rimmed glasses, and rang up the purchase on a cash register, which stood among an array of bottles whose labels had faded to a uniform café au lait. Above them dust gathered on the ridges and grooves of an elaborately engraved mirror.

'Where you headed?' she asked as I stuffed away my change.

191

'North.'

'Up 52?'

I nodded.

She flicked up her eyebrows. 'Good luck.' She chuckled hoarsely. 'What you drivin'?'

'A Bronco.'

She turned away, picked up a pack of Winston. 'You should be all right. Take it easy, that's all.' She pulled out a fresh cigarette.

It was a strange day. I had to ford a number of muddy rivers first, where I popped the Bronco into four-wheel drive, then finally we rose into big open country, Marlboro country, and began to climb. I could see the track heading off into the distance, looping up over far ridges like in a cartoon.

Once an old Dodge saloon came crawling up towards me. A drunken cowboy leaned out the window and told me I had sixty-odd miles to go before I hit pavement again. He held up a bottle of Bud and tipped it into his mouth. Even over the gurgle of the idling Bronco I heard the roar of his huge engine as he rolled on up the hill. I went slowly, passing the time by listening to Country and Western songs on the radio. One reminded me of the fisherman I had worked for in Maine years before. It was called 'Get Yourself a Working Man's PhD'. It was an attack on college boys. They had been one of the fisherman's pet hates too, and while working for him I had done my best to conceal my credentials.

Then I started experimenting with the jar of Religious Experience hot sauce. I took it out of the glove box and jammed it between my legs, tearing open the bag of tortilla chips with my teeth, and endeavoured to convert myself. It wasn't easy. At first if I dipped so much as the corner of a chip even in the film of liquid that had formed on the surface of the salsa, I scalded my mouth, and had to eat a handful of neat chips to dilute the pain. But something always drew me back. Irresistibly, it seemed, I would prod the corner of another big triangular chip into the sauce, and burn myself again. Yet I kept doing it. It was partly curiosity, to see how much of this heat I could endure, and partly the knowledge that all over the world people enjoyed the sensation, so presumably there must be something in it, and partly the rumour I had heard that chilli had a mild narcotic effect. What better place, I reasoned, than a big old four-wheel-drive truck and a colossal empty landscape for a mild narcotic effect? But I wasn't getting the effect, and I kept coming back for more till I did.

I forgot how it happened. The transition occurred imperceptibly. As far as I could remember afterwards, one minute I was still dipping corners of chips into the fiery oil on the surface, and the next I was scooping the chips down into the jar and shovelling out mouthfuls of the red sauce itself. The insidious pain was there still but something had come over me. I couldn't stop myself from wanting more of it. The chilli frenzy had come upon me. I could think of nothing but the jar between my thighs, and mechanically, like a hypnotist's stooge, I kept on scooping up mouthful after mouthful.

The spell broke when I brought a chip up to my mouth and found it empty. I looked down to discover that I had eaten half the jar. I sat with my mouth open while my gums sweated out all the fire, feeling the knocks and jolts and shudderings of the Bronco making its way over the long track, hearing the incessant squeal of its plastic cab roof shivering against its mouldings, and gazed ahead in a kind of trance. I felt numbed and calm, insulated from my surroundings. So this was the chilli narcosis, I reflected. I stopped to have a pee in a pine copse at the bottom of a vast valleyside. I put the jar up on top of the dash and climbed out, suddenly aware of my now weathered suede boots, feeling surprised and delighted, as if I had won a triumphant victory over myself. I had tough suede boots, drove a Bronco and could eat as much chilli as I liked. I had conquered the fire.

The track turned to mud once again. I slithered along, held on course by deep ruts. I wondered how the cowboy in the Dodge could have made this stretch, and guessed he must have cut up onto the track from some farm. Then I was climbing again, up a tremendous open hill, with here and there a fan of gaunt rocks rising out of it like the dorsal plates of some dinosaur. To the right the land fell in a sweep of dry grass. To the left it lifted up to a furrow of black woods nested in against the foot of a grey cliff, which soared up into the cloudy sky, stained with black smears like the gutter stains on London brickwork. It was a cathedral of a landscape, but nothing to what I saw once the track had carried me to the shoulder of the hillside, and I peered over the brow. Beyond lay a vast valley, a valley so big it seemed a world unto itself. It tumbled down in a range of hills and climbed again far off, faintly, in a haze of blue and yellow land. It must have been sunny over there, while here we still stewed under a blanket of white cloud.

That valley was what I had to cross. The sight of it made me check the petrol gauge, which mercifully was still on three-quarters full. I had met the cowboy some ten miles back. It seemed unlikely the pavement would start again before I reached the far side, but that looked like it could be even further than another fifty miles.

I jammed the jar of hot sauce against the windshield, set on its side for ease of access, and let my foot off the brake. It was a long slow ride. Once I saw two deer cantering across the slope far away. Then I thought I saw a black rock move, close to some trees. I could have sworn it moved. I thought it must have been a bear. I stopped and watched it a long time, but it didn't move again.

I hit a brief, intense rainstorm so powerful it left the track pockmarked as if it had been pelted with a hail of tiny meteorites.

It was mid afternoon when a series of switchbacks carried me up the last bare slope to a saddle-shaped pass. I rattled over a cattle-grid and the track suddenly changed from mud and rocks to even white, and I found myself on level ground. The tyres hissed as I picked up speed. The gravel ribbon made a slow even bend to the left, a big turn such as a boat would describe, around a crest, then headed dead straight across a flat, barren khaki plain – a perfect level desert encircled by the mountains. I wondered why it was suddenly such a well-maintained track, and was surprised to see a road sign travelling towards me, a small green sign with a white border. I was even more surprised to read what it said. Without any explanation, it declared: 'A Very Large Array'.

What did that mean? I wondered if it might be some post-modern poem erected out here in the middle of nowhere by a landscape artist, or else some kind of military code. I knew large tracts of New Mexican wilderness were used by the military. Or this could have been a huge empty township, and I had just crossed the boundary, and that was its odd name. It was hardly any odder than Truth or Consequences, after all. Far away, somewhere on the other side of the plain, it seemed, I could make out what appeared to be a cluster of small white shapes. I wondered what they were, and if the strange road sign could have anything to do with them. They looked like the white domes and minarets of a mosque in the desert. Then all of a sudden, without any warning, a railway track started up alongside me. No buffers, no fence, not even a pile of gravel: the rails simply began right there, resting on their ladder of concrete sleepers. What was a railway line doing out here? It looked neat and well maintained too.

I began to get the feeling that I was somewhere I wasn't supposed to be – something like James Bond trespassing on Spectre's head-quarters and realizing it too late, knowing that by now all their closed-circuit TVs would have picked him up and gun barrels would be trained on him. I had the feeling I had walked into an ambush. Everything seemed unnaturally still. I wouldn't have been altogether surprised if a helicopter had suddenly swung into view in front of me and a man with a megaphone had boomed down at me to stop the car and throw away my keys.

The white shapes didn't grow for a long time. Then suddenly I looked up and they seemed to be a fleet of white sailing boats. Was there a lake up here? Then I noticed a grey block in the middle of them. Was it some strange kind of airport, I wondered, and that

195

was the control tower, and the white shapes were some odd desert aircraft I had never seen before. It got me wondering about that road sign again. A very large array of *what*?

They must still have been a mile off when I finally saw what they were: satellite dishes. It was a cluster of bright white radio dishes. The railway line was still there beside me, and the road and rails obviously both led to them.

But I was wrong about the distance: I still had some three miles to go. It was an easy mistake to make: they were enormous dishes, I was to discover, among the biggest in the world, each one some 150 feet high. Not only that, but there were no fewer than thirty of them, each one set on its own giant railway car ready to be transported to any point along the railway track. And there were in fact three such tracks, three great radii laid out on the plain, each one thirteen miles long.

I turned off the gravel and followed a short paved road to the concrete house in the middle, where a sign directed me to the Visitors' Center.

'Welcome to the Very Large Array,' a board declared, 'Part of the World's Largest Telescope.' I parked the Bronco in the car park.

Inside was a small, unlit museum with no one around. There were display cases and posters on the walls, all set up to explain what this place was: namely one of the few 'Very Large Array Telescopes'. There were six of them in all, strung across America, from the Virgin Islands to Hawaii. They were radio-wave rather than light-wave telescopes, but could provide visual images of the cosmos, and by using a number of dishes they could achieve powers of magnification that otherwise would require vast dishes many miles in diameter. Not only that, but all six VLA telescopes could in fact be linked together by computer, and thus form the 'Very Long Baseline Telescope', which was the most powerful telescope in the world. For one single radio dish to have been as powerful it would have had to have been two hundred and seventy miles wide, a poster informed me. 'Hardly practical!' joked the scientist who had written the blurb.

Most of the posters were lurid pictures of nebulae and gas explosions and red giants, or fallen suns, and blurry moons in far-off galaxies. The messages boasted that the team here could fill their lens with a dime left on the moon. Details of solar systems a hundred or a thousand light years away were routine matters for them. In the twelve years they had been here they had both solved and unearthed more riddles of the cosmos than had ever been thought possible. The cards didn't actually list these triumphs, but I found it easy to take them on faith.

I went out to look around. A path led over to the dishes, and other paths led to various small buildings, perhaps laboratories or storerooms or accommodation for the team of astrophysicists and technicians. It was like a space-station on the moon: a wildly remote encampment, an outpost of science stranded on a treeless planet.

I wandered down the first path. Seated on the carriage of the nearest dish, with one foot up on the iron deck, was a man in a khaki satin flying jacket and a blue skiing hat. It wasn't particularly cold, but there was thin cloud cover veiling the sun, and it struck me that it was a good day on which to be wearing a warm hat. The man lifted a hand off his knee by way of a wave. He had a silver-grey stubble on his jaw, a black moustache and beady, laughing eyes.

'First time?' he asked.

'Yes.'

He paused. 'What do you think?' He smiled, like a father showing off a new car to his son.

'Incredible.'

'It is incredible. And the most incredible thing of all, you know what they are doing right now? You know what's going on right now on this *thing* here?' He glanced up at the vast curved sheet that gleamed above us, lifting into the sky. 'You know what?'

'No.'

'They're not looking at stars and nebulae and gases and stuff. None of that. Sure, they do a little of that now and then to keep everyone happy and quiet, but you know what's really going down?'

I wondered who this man was. There was an Isuzu Trooper II parked in the lot, and I assumed it must be his, but somehow he seemed a little too settled in here to be a visitor. He was more like a worker having a day off, or someone on night shift taking it easy in the afternoon. I figured he might have been one of the engineers or electricians that they presumably had to employ.

'You ever stop to ask yourself why New Mexico has the highest rate of UFO sightings in the world? You ever think about that, or what you can do with the world's most powerful radio transmitter? You could call up the Andromeda Galaxy and have a talk as clear as you and me talking on the telephone. There'd be a slight time-lag problem, but hell, what would *you* do with a thing like that? You'd talk, right? What else do you do with a telephone?'

'You mean they don't use this as a telescope?'

'Sure they do. But also as a megaphone.' He chuckled. 'A megaphone pointed at the cosmos. "Is anybody out there?" That's what they yell. As many different ways as they can think of. "We're here! Are you there?"'

'You think they've heard anything back yet?'

'Are you *kidding*? They've been sending out their greetings every which way for twelve years, they're gonna have started getting in some replies.' He laughed again.

There was something about the sparkle in his eyes that made me feel he must be right, he knew what he was talking about. I wanted to believe him. But I asked, 'If they have heard, why don't they let on?'

'Think about it.'

I did, for a moment, and came up with nothing.

'They talk, they bring down the entire socio-economic fabric of our society. Can you imagine the chaos if they announced there were space fleets from Andromeda coming to say hi?'

I didn't answer. I couldn't imagine it. I also wondered if I was talking to a nut, perhaps a man who had once worked here and flipped out. Except that he seemed convincingly reasonable. And I wondered why it would be the Andromeda, of all galaxies, which I knew to be one of the most distant. I asked him this.

'Parallel universe.'

'What?'

'Andromeda. Theory is, it's a parallel universe.'

I knew so little about modern physics that I wasn't sure if this was some crank's notion or some genuine Einsteinian feat of cosmic acrobatics. Certainly I could remember a Star Trek episode where they visited a parallel universe. But I doubted that that meant the notion was rooted in orthodoxy.

'Ah,' I said, inclining to the view that I was talking to some victim of cabin fever, say, or of too many Arthur C. Clarke books. There was a moment of silence.

'You work here?' I asked.

He shook his head. 'No, no. I'm a sculptor. Been to Santa Fe?'

'Yes.'

'Seen my works on the Paseo?'

'Paseo de Peralta?' I had indeed seen a number of sculptures on the central reservation of Paseo de Peralta, mostly large metal devices, some painted in bold colours, others bare and crudely welded.

'You seen my totems?'

I remembered a series of odd totem-pole-like creations made out of pieces of metal.

He nodded. 'Uh-huh. That's them. Made them out of disused bomb parts from Los Alamos Weapons Laboratory.'

'Nuclear bomb parts?'

'Sure, but they're safe. They decontaminate them before they sell them off. Fine metals, they are. Hard to get.'

'Like what?'

'Like tungsten, titanium, vanadium. You try and get pure vanadium in your local hardware.' He let out a rattling laugh.

We fell silent again. He gazed off over the plain.

'So what brings you here?' I asked.

'Me? I like to come up here from time to time. Just come up here and *be*. It gets me thinking about things.' He nodded, looking away again at the far mountains. 'This is a good spot. A fine place just to be.'

I sighed and agreed and thought about the endless universe and whether there was compassionate life out in it and if they knew about us and would one day come and visit. With the great white disc above and the empty plain all around, it certainly seemed a fine place to think about such things.

Before I left he walked me over to the parking lot. 'Take a look at this.' He opened up his Isuzu Trooper and pulled out a copy of a magazine called *The Journal of the Crop Circle*. He turned to a page in the middle.

I stood there for a minute reading about two warring bands of aliens who were fighting over the earth. I thought at first it was a piece of science fiction, but it became clear that the author intended it as a piece of news reporting. Apparently there was a gene shortage in the universe and the earth had been established as a gene bank a long time ago. That was what we were all doing here. We were a glass tank in a biology lab, a culture on a slide. That explained why people got abducted periodically: so the extraterrestrials could conduct genetic experiments. Now the gene bank was ripening and the original founders, who were good beings, were finding themselves challenged by a malicious gang called the Betas, who planned to steal the store of genes.

'Interesting,' I said, handing it back.

He chuckled significantly. 'Man, you're standing in one of the epicentres.' He glanced up. 'That sky up there, I guess it's pretty busy right now.'

'The war over New Mexico?' I offered.

'You could put it that way.' He nodded slowly. 'You could put it that way.'

He flipped the magazine onto his car seat. 'Well, if I don't see you around up in Santa Fe, perhaps I'll see you on another plane one of these days.'

I opened up the Bronco and eased myself up onto the high seat. I turned the key. The truck shook comfortably awake. 'I hope so,' I said.

He saluted me. 'All power to the highway, wherever it takes us.'

I nodded, and slipped the beast into gear. I let it roll slowly out along the driveway, slowly enough to watch the sculptor as he walked back down the path towards the first of the giant radio dishes. I saw him resume his post, and wondered if he hoped that by being so close he might somehow pick up the radio waves himself, and listen in on one of those phantom conversations – be one of the first civilians to overhear a dialogue with an alien. He struck me just then as a happy man, not deluded at all. The universe was infinite, there must be other life in it, and it wasn't such a bad aim to want to know about it. And there was something expansive about him, something cosmic. He wasn't cramped, he gave himself a lot of space. That was the sense he gave when you saw him perched there beneath the great dish: not desperate at all, but patient.

EIGHTEEN

Floods at Dusk

IT WAS FOUR O'CLOCK when I hit Route 66, some ten miles away. I was pleased to find myself on the world's most famous road, but just there it was an empty two-lane road with no traffic. It carried me out of the great basin of the Very Large Array and wound eastwards through the mountains, dropping down their eastern flanks onto the central plain. I passed through Datil, a tiny hamlet of five clapboard houses, one of them a closed-up general store, and through Magdalena, then reached the town of Socorro and the interstate highway.

By now it was six o'clock. A fine sunset was thickening behind me, the sky like orange juice above the purple silhouette of the mountains. I caught glimpses of it in the mirror every time I rounded a bend. I had been planning to head straight on up the highway and roll into Las Vegas tonight. I estimated it would be a three-hour drive: two up to the Santa Fe exits, then another hour along the Freeway heading east. That would put me there at nine o'clock, in time to get a room at the Plaza Hotel, an old hotel I had heard about right on the plaza. But I figured it might be cutting it fine, and I was in no hurry. It had been a long day already, and besides, something else made me decide to spend the night in Socorro: a road sign, painted in brown to indicate a site of local interest, to a place called 'El Bosque del Apache', eight miles from Socorro.

I had heard about El Bosque before. It was a nature reserve where snowy cranes rested in the middle of their autumn migration from Canada to Mexico. Thousands upon thousands of the birds flocked to the waters and marshlands of El Bosque each evening and morning. A friend had raved at some length about the spectacle they formed, and here it was only eight miles away. I pictured something like you might see in the pages of *National Geographic*, blizzards of birds filling the sky.

I passed through the main strip of town and soon found myself on a small road elevated between two ditches. A guard stepped out of a wooden hut at the gate into the reserve and took five dollars off me. I studied a map on a board for a moment, saw the track within formed a big loop, and took my foot off the brake.

Now, after two days of continuous cross-country use, the Bronco had cleared its throat and settled down. It purred along contentedly as I crept over the dirt track, making the drop into second gear with a smooth, barely perceptible change in pitch. It felt as if the driving had made the truck cohere better, as if it had loosened up like an athlete and now could move with a single easy purpose. Warm, loose, gurgling evenly, the high square bonnet shaking gently over the bumps in the track, the cab roof squealing less intensely now, it was a pleasure to drive. I hadn't looked, but I imagined the bodywork must have been covered in dried dirt, like a rally car, and that too added to the joy of it, especially at the end of the day, when the sunset was bathing everything in the golden light of an epiphany. I imagined the truck with all its dust and dirt looking like some sandy-golden victor of the Paris–Dakar.

Meanwhile I had not yet hit any snowfields of roosting white birds. Here and there a dotted line of homeward-bound geese moved across the sky, the line wavering slightly, as if passing through a liquid medium. I drove by a ploughed field across which a scattered troop of wild turkeys strutted, pecking at the grain. Then a lone coyote appeared, a dim pale shape pausing at the far side of the field. It took a few steps towards the turkeys and paused again. One of the birds looked up, erecting its neck like a periscope into the clear evening air, swivelling it jerkily, then commenced a slow, measured run towards the track I was on. Half-way to the hedge it began to flap its wings, which it had been holding open, bent at the elbows. Noisily, with a clapping of feathers and a gurgled alarm call, it drew itself aloft and flapped right over me. The coyote began to run. One by one the turkeys caught on. Soon the field was alive with a jangling chorus of falsetto gurgles and with what now seemed an avalanche of rolling boulders and flapping wings. There were far more birds than I had noticed at first, camouflaged against the earth. It seemed the coyote had made a wise choice for its hunting-ground. Surely of the hundreds of birds that now grew like a hallucination out of the ploughed sod there would be one sick or wounded.

But it wasn't its night. It must have been weary with hunger, or else some gene had made coyotes careful not to squander their energy. Either way, before it was half-way to the rolling, fluttering earth, when a number of birds were still only just pricking up their heads to look about, and I was looking forward to witnessing a full *National Geographic* hunting spread being enacted before my eyes, the coyote gave up. It apparently knew better, and needed more surprise than three hundred yards of bare earth could offer. It began a mournful retreat back to the far edge of the field, head held low.

Twilight was falling and still I had seen no sign of the cranes. Tall red rushes flanked the track now. Through them the western sky looked a luminous green. The air was cooler, you could just taste the slow start of winter in it, and very clear. Every tree, every reed, every leaf seemed to stand out and rise to meet your vision. Of the shallow lakes I passed now and then, the ones to the east were dark and sombre, lightless gulfs in the land, while those beneath the western sky were brilliant mirrors, chrome sheets lying still, calm, unblemished among the rushes.

I drove through a copse of trees that were already losing their leaves, their bare twigs looking rusty in the late light, and when I came out, far off, on the other side of a lake, I could see a column of yellow smoke rising into the sunset, dust put up by a silver truck glinting at the front. Between myself and that truck the water's surface was thickly studded with what looked like heaps of snow. I wound down the window and switched off the truck. Suddenly the evening filled with the cackles and honks of what I thought were geese, but so many of them calling all at once that the effect was like the incomprehensible babble of a vast cocktail party.

These were the snowy cranes, and now that the sun had gone down I noticed more of them approaching overhead in flocks big enough to darken the sky like small clouds, and in far-off V-formations, which looked like thin trails of steam. When these packs arrived the din would increase, as the birds suddenly opened out their wings as wide as they could, ready for landing, and hovered about searching for vacant roosts in the shallow water. Gradually the surface filled, until there hardly seemed to be any space left at all. Yet more and more kept coming, evidently drawn by the magnetic force of the congregation. It made me think about cities and the drive that impelled humans to crowd themselves into restricted spaces. This was evidently something similar: the intense excitement of participating in such a throng, and of adding one's voice to the great chorus of cries so similar to one's own, the dizzy intoxication of the great party, was evidently far more compelling than the placid emptiness of the neighbouring lake, on which they could have chosen any roost they liked.

I got out of the car and waited, watching. I didn't know specifically what I was waiting for – perhaps for night to fall, perhaps for all the cranes to quieten down and go to sleep, or perhaps I was hoping they would all suddenly rise up into the sky in one great commotion of flashing white – but it felt good to be out there by the water, so close to the city of birds, with dark creeping in. The surface was still bright and metallic among the birds, but the mountains were a smoky shape now, weak, as if they had faded like a pair of jeans in too many washes, and the sky was settling down into a deep blue sheen. Behind me the copse I had driven through had become a formless smudge.

As I sat on my haunches, watching the sky darken over the cranes in the middle of the empty landscape of central New Mexico, I found myself thinking about evenings back home in England. There were flood meadows where I grew up, and each year in early winter the Canal Authority would open the sluices and our walks would turn into flat, still lakes, sheets of water that caught the low evening light the same way these waters had done. We would button up our coats and wrap scarves round our necks, feel the cold numb our noses and watch the dogs making ripples at the edge of the silver water. I remembered the feeling of knowing that the house was not far away, that though it was cold and clear and winter was making its magnificent entrance, and we were out witnessing it, soon we would be sitting on the floor beside a fire of noisy green wood, smelling the sap, waiting for dinner.

These childhood memories made me homesick now. I wondered what I was doing in the desert of New Mexico. The land here was beautiful, it was fascinating and spectacular, but it wasn't mine. The fact was, I did have a land of my own, but this wasn't it. I remembered how fragile and delicate England could be, its beauty intensified by knowing that I had a life in it, that it had once been my whole world.

Gradually the cranes quietened down, hooking their bills between their wings in the middle of their backs, their necks curving round like the handles of old silver teapots. The sky in the west stayed bright, but overhead stars appeared. Then a pair of headlights flashed on me and a truck gurgled up the track, stopping beside me. It was the guard. He said they were closing up.

I climbed back into the Bronco. As I drove back towards Socorro through the darkening landscape, my mood slowly lifted. I reminded myself that however much I already thought this journey to New Mexico had given me, it would be years before I fully digested its benefits. Travelling was like bringing in the stores: it would be a long time before this voyage's nourishment wore off, and it might never wear off.

I spent the night in a Lucky Eight motel on the edge of town, and ate a steak in the old Valverde Steakhouse.

'How would you like it?' the young, cheerful, fat-cheeked waitress asked me, her hair a mass of ringlets.

'Medium rare.'

'Red, green or Christmas?' she asked, scribbling away on her pad.

'What?'

'Christmas, red or green?'

'What's that?'

'What's what?' She looked up from her pad, smiled.

'What's any of that?'

She nodded, as if she now understood that I didn't understand. 'Uh-huh. That's chilli sauce. Red or green or both?'

I hesitated. 'Both, I guess.'

It was an old restaurant, a brick building with viga beams in the ceiling and carved wooden doors. Decades ago it had been the main hotel in town, till the motels drove it into its present retreat as a restaurant. But it was a good place to sit alone. It was mostly empty tonight, but I was enjoying the pampering that ordinary American restaurants offer. The waitress came back with a basket of soft rolls, a saucer of whipped butter and a frozen mug of dark Mexican beer. Then a bus-boy put a glass of ice on the table, and filled it with water from his pitcher. A salad appeared, which apparently came with my steak, along with four bottles of dressing: a pink one called French, an orange one called Russian, a white Italian and a thick, creamy 'Rancho'. I tried a little of each, pouring them out on opposite sides of my oval salad plate, working them in towards the centre as I ate. They were all variations on the triple theme of mayonnaise, tomato ketchup and sugar, but they tasted delicious. The rolls were good too, fluffy and soft and easy to tear open.

But I wasn't ready for the steak. First the waitress brought over a folding table similar to the suitcase-stand devices in hotel rooms, followed by a steak knife, which she inserted at the appropriate place in my cutlery, namely across the top. Then she brought out a carving-board with a large piece of meat. I assumed that, as in an English carvery, she would carve me off my slice, but she proceeded to cut the whole thing into a series of ten neat steaks, each one a good size in itself, and lay them out carefully on an oversized serving dish, which turned out to be my plate. She disappeared, then re-emerged with a large bowl of French fries and a soup bowl filled with a red and a green sauce that met in a neat line in the middle. She spooned out some of each for me, blurring the line.

It was good steak, pink and tender, but I couldn't eat half of it. It was a long time before she came to take away my plate, asking, 'You're sure now?' twice, before she would remove it. Then she asked how I wanted my apple pie, 'a la mode' or with whipped cream.

'My apple pie?'

'Uh-huh. Salad and sweet come with a steak. We got cherry pie too but our apple pie is famous.' She laughed modestly.

I sighed. 'I guess I better try it then.'

'And how would you like that?' she repeated.

I shrugged. 'A la mode.'

It came with two huge balls of ice-cream perched on top. I managed to eat a couple of mouthfuls, then asked for a coffee.

I slept well that night. It wasn't a new mattress, in fact it was lumpy and sagged, evidently limp from years of clandestine battering, but I didn't wake up till after the orange glow of street lamps on the curtains had turned to the even pallor of daylight.

And I woke up excited. I was finally going to Las Vegas, New Mexico. There was nothing now between me and Vegas, just three hours of highway. I stuffed my spare clothes into my bag, zipped it up, and paced out to the Bronco in my boots, which were stiff after their night's rest. I thrummed gently over to the motel office, then cruised along the town strip at the pace of a kerb-crawler, looking for a cup of coffee. I stopped in at a Dunkin' Donuts, and growled out of town with a white paper bag of breakfast on the seat beside me. It was a good way to start the day, sipping from a cup of coffee over the steering wheel, hearing the purr of the great engine as it gathered speed, and all around, outside the windows, the empty desert lying gentle and tired still, as if aching in its muscles after the dewless night, beneath a talcum-white sky. A surge of anticipation ran through me. I remembered mornings working for the fisherman in Maine. Every day at three o'clock, when it was still dark, we drove down to the dock where the boat was moored, stopping in at the gas station to buy a twelve-pack of donuts and a pair of chilli dogs, then rowed out to the boat in the dinghy as the sun rose into the blue world like a slow balloon. I thought of the airport in Vermont where I had worked too, and rattling down the tracks off the hills in the morning as it got light, with a plastic beaker of coffee in one hand and the steering wheel in the other, skidding on the ribs in the dirt and holding the cup away from me so it wouldn't scald my legs. And here I was now once more having breakfast on the road in America. That was what had excited me about those other mornings: being out on the land of America. The American land seemed at those early hours to possess a vital energy all its own, something clean and pure and powerful which you sensed as you watched the dips and curves and contours of the road ahead. It seemed to travel up through your feet and infect your whole body with its rhythm. It made you feel yourself a lucky creature: lucky to be alive, lucky to be an animal walking upright on the earth, lucky to be able to notice that you were both those things.

NINETEEN

The Skies over New Mexico

THE MAN IN THE BOOKSTORE assured me it was genuine: a copy of a photobiography of Cary Grant autographed by the actor himself. 'For Gaby,' it said, 'As ever, love, Cary.' It answered a question that had always puzzled me: did he call himself Cary or Archibald among his personal friends? But I still didn't know what his passport said: A. Leach, Esq., born Bristol, UK? I didn't even know if he had a British passport.

It got me thinking: quite a number of Brits had come out west to LA and stayed. It wasn't such a strange thing to do, even though the west was so different from Britain. The west was different from everywhere. It was a virgin land, in spirit. It was foreign to everyone, even to Americans, and open to everyone, a new land on which you could inscribe the shape of your own independent life. As I drove north earlier in the day I had daydreamed again about staying out here, imagining how I would do it: I could rent a flat, I could try for a teaching job up at the college outside Santa Fe, perhaps even buy the Bronco. I tried to compare that life with the vestigial life I had back home, but it was hard. It was like trying to compare a bowl of fresh, rinsed fruit with a fruitless cherry tree in winter: which was better? How could you say? The first was better for right now, clearly, but it seemed like a betrayal to shift one's allegiance from the long quiet growth of the second. I thought of examples of people I knew who had migrated: a distant cousin, a car-painter, had emigrated from Finchley to Australia when I was a child. It had been a big family event, though we had seldom seen him or his children. He was a clan hero for having once painted Tom Jones's Rolls-Royce.

The man in the bookstore wanted fifty dollars for the Cary Grant book, which was nothing more than a slim expanded fanzine. I put it back on the display table and wandered deeper into the shop. It was a strange store, a long narrow flimsily built room with boxes of books waiting to be unpacked, probably bought as lots at garage sales, and shelves sagging along the walls. In the back there was a kind of café divided into three parts, one with an old cappuccino machine and tables coated in coloured plastic, another equipped with a row of leather booths, and the third a kind of dilapidated conservatory full of board games and chess sets. All three parts were deserted. The furthest one terminated in a glass door onto the next street: you could walk through the entire store from one street to the other. In effect, the store formed a covered alleyway across the block, though it didn't look like anyone had used it either as an alley or as a café, or even as a bookstore, in a long time.

The owner was a middle-aged man with a great head of ginger hair, which he kept brushed back, but which, being stiff and recalcitrant, rose up in a defiant wave at the front, before giving in and retreating. He wore thick glasses and had a long round-ended nose. As he spoke he snorted in the back of his head between words, as if attempting to clear his sinuses.

'Excuse me, sir,' he called to me.

I had had the feeling when I entered that I was the first person to have been in that day, perhaps even that week. It wasn't just the shop itself, which had an air of utter neglect, but also the street outside. It was the main shopping street of Las Vegas, leading from the bridge over the river directly up to the plaza, flanked by commercial premises for three blocks. But many of these were boarded up, and most of those that weren't were junk shops – big spaces with iron pillars supporting their roofs and high brick fronts such as you see in cowboy films, their interiors littered, more than stocked, with a variety of debris from all manner of fallen enterprises: everything from the sad waste of collapsed households – old cookers, worn shiny sofas, sets of interlocking blackened pans – to old Gulf petrol pumps from bankrupt service stations leaning against the wall, and incomplete ratchet sets still in the cardboard boxes in which they had been hurriedly thrown. You could find crates of delicious-sounding lotions from abandoned New Age herbal stores – avocado and lemon face creams, cherry and orange body oils, strawberry and melon bath gels, all long past their sell-by dates – and baskets of multi-coloured crystals to improve the atmosphere in the home. Here and there you came across old iron mining implements and old gardening tools with broken handles. It seemed a desperate street: the shops were being used effectively as garages or attics, with the doors kept unlocked most days just in case someone happened to go by who might relieve them of something or other, anything, and see fit to pay a little money besides. It wasn't a ghost town. Far from it. Some forty thousand people lived in the old wood houses on its grid of leafy streets. But it was commercially dead.

'Excuse me,' the owner of the bookstore repeated, stepping out from behind the table he used as a counter. I turned to face him.

'I think you might perhaps be interested in this.' He made the noise in the back of his nose again and pushed up his glasses.

I examined the shelf he was indicating. Sure enough, it was interesting: a shelf full of early American editions of James Bond books.

'Here.' He got down on his knees, which cracked just before they hit the floor, and began pulling out books here and there till he had a stack of old Signet paperbacks, all from the 1960s. 'Complete set. All twelve books.' He held the pile out to me.

A little reluctantly I took the books and flipped through them. They all had one of Ian Fleming's various extravagant publicity shots on the back: smouldering at the camera, a long cigarette holder between his fingers and a curl of smoke half obscuring his face; clad in a lavish cravat; sneering with narrowed eyes at the reader, as if scornfully challenging him to dare open the book.

The man asked twenty-five dollars, then dropped his price to fifteen, and finally, as I left, to one dollar apiece. I didn't particularly want to carry them about with me, but it seemed ungrateful not to buy them at that price. He tipped the neat stack haphazardly into a used plastic bag from the A and P supermarket as soon as I agreed.

Las Vegas was a strange town. For one thing it was unnaturally quiet. There was hardly anyone about on the streets. Now and then an old pickup truck would go by. The plaza, a large square with big trees, an iron bandstand, and surrounded by old brick houses all built with those high western fronts, was permanently deserted. Even the Plaza Hotel where I was staying, a grand old western-style hotel with shutters on the windows, a restaurant with wood and wicker furniture, a big chandelier in the hallway – all the fittings and furnishings dating from the turn of the century, when Las Vegas had been at the centre of a prosperous ranching country – was empty. The morning I arrived the hotel had just been vacated by a convention of the Federation of New Mexican Music Teachers, and now I was the only guest in its fifty rooms.

But the town was a good place for a solitary traveller. It had an oppressed air, which is just what a lone roamer needs in order to feel unoppressed himself. I passed the day comfortably. I sat in my room with the shutters open, watching red leaves spin to the ground in the square when gusts blew. I sat in the saloon bar downstairs listening to the one man in the bar, a local with a bushy black beard, chubby, his thighs stuffed into a pair of boyish blue jeans, attempt to chat up the barmaid, a blonde girl with a coat of bronzing make-up on her cheeks, and her hair enamelled by hair-spray into a stiff motionless bob. I strolled up and down the empty streets. I drank cups of coffee in the two empty diners in town, one of which doubled strangely as a Chinese restaurant. The juke-box was full of *Música Norteña* from Mexico and Tex-Mex classics such as 'Adios Mexico' by the Texas Tornados, a song that the waitress kept playing over and over again till I had it so firmly implanted in my mind that months later I found myself singing snatches of the refrain. Yet the walls were adorned with Chinese fans and parasols, and the back page of the menu offered chop sueys and fu yungs and sizzling Szechuan dishes. I walked along an old railway line out of town till it crossed a bloated grey river wrinkled into elephant hide by the eddies in its swift current. I rested my elbows on the parapet of an old iron bridge and studied the decorative brickwork of a disused factory on the far bank, and thought of England, and the old backwaters of industry that you could find tucked away like this in most British towns.

As I idled away my time I pondered what to do. What preoccupied me was the Flying Father. As far as I knew I was in his home town now. This was my chance to see him, yet each time I contemplated getting into the Bronco to make my tour of the town churches to see if I could raise him, or at least find out his current whereabouts, I hesitated. Once I got as far as locking myself in the wooden-doored telephone cubicle under the stairs in the hotel and opening up the directory, a thin book with a picture of Thompson Peak, a local mountain, on the cover. I found the Las Vegas section, but no Bertoni was listed. I tried the yellow pages at the back, under Religious Assemblies. There was a whole column of churches, at least half of them in Las Vegas. I could have diligently dialled my way down the list, but I held back from doing it.

What bothered me most was the reluctance I seemed to feel towards actually searching for him. I didn't understand it. This was it. I was in Las Vegas. Why didn't I start calling? Or else jump in the Bronco and cruise around from church to church and check the notice-boards outside until I found him? The church boards always gave the names of the preachers. Sooner or later I would inevitably come across him. Then I could try to find his telephone number with directory enquiries. Or perhaps I would run into a verger or churchkeeper of some kind who would point me to the Padre's house.

But supposing I did – supposing I found myself standing at the end of the Flying Father's drive and there was a light on in the sitting room and a car parked in the driveway. What then? What kind of car would it be, for a start? A small Honda, a big old gas-guzzler, a Jeep, an anonymous Ford? I decided it wouldn't matter to him at all, a car for him could be nothing more than a utility for his mission in life. And if I knocked on the door how would I know it was him? Suppose he had let his hair grow, or grown a beard? And what would I say? And above all, now that I was here, what was the point? I was in New Mexico, I had joined that obscure brotherhood of people who had been to New Mexico. The place had worked its magic on me. I could still feel the door that had opened up inside me in Taos swinging free. The peace I had found within, across its threshold, in Santa Fe was still glowing away all by itself. What did I need the Flying Father for? What could I tell him? What could I show him? What did I really have to say to him?

And suppose he didn't fly any more? Suppose he had got fat and spent the evenings with his wife in front of the TV? Who could blame him if he did? Vigour was limited in everyone. You couldn't be a gaunt pilot all your life. I might arrive as an unwelcome reminder of his former life.

It was a Friday. I had promised the owner of the Bronco that I would bring it back on Monday. I figured I might as well use it as long as I could, so I didn't rush back to Santa Fe. That night I went along to a bar on the edge of town called Murillo's (pronounced more or less like *morellos*) and drank a couple of beers. It was crowded with Hispanic men, and as soon as I walked in I could feel it was a rough joint. Later I discovered it was nicknamed 'Cuchillo's', after its clientele's propensity for knife fights. Two plump waitresses dressed in tight skirts fixed beers and tequilas along the counter. There weren't many other women in the place. What few there were sat with gangs of men at the tables, and were all small and thoroughly made up. They didn't look like prostitutes, but they did look like they would make feisty partners for the beer-swilling men who were buying their drinks.

As soon as I reached the bar I felt several pairs of eyes fasten on me. They came from further along the bar, and something told me not to look back. It was hard to resist the temptation, and I could only do it by reading over and over again the 'Joke of the Week', written up in fluorescent blue on a blackboard behind the bar: 'Question: Why do gay men smoke cigars? Answer: Practice.'

It was such a poor joke that for a while I wasn't sure I had got it. I was tempted to glance around the room to see if anyone was smoking a cigar – I thought this joke might be provocation enough for a fight to break out – but managed to restrain myself.

I quietly drank a Dos Equis at the bar, picking at the label until it suddenly occurred to me that in an establishment such as this fiddling with your beer bottle might conceivably be construed to be as camp as cigar-smoking, and tried to wipe the frayed edges of the gold paper back down. There was a salad bowl full of popcorn on the bar, and now and then I allowed my fingers to make a discreet foray into it. No one seemed to mind that. Gradually I felt myself blending in.

I began to reflect. This was northern New Mexico, right on the frontier of the old Spanish colonies. New Mexico had been sold to America along with Texas in 1867, but only recently had its Anglo population begun to swell significantly. In a town like this it was still a Hispanic land. Not only that, but from here you could travel south uninterrupted all the way to Tierra del Fuego without speaking a word of English or eating a mouthful of English food, if you didn't want to. This, in effect, was the far-flung edge of the Spanish world. Mexico was four hours away by car. From the border you could pass all the way down the isthmus of Central America into

South America, and all the way down the Andes or through the Amazon and into the tapering tail of the continent. I was sitting on the edge of New Spain.

But also at the end of it.

It hadn't occurred to me before, but now I saw a simple design behind the travelling I had done over the years. My first trip, made when I was eighteen, had taken me from Argentina, in the south of the continent, up to Ecuador. The second one, made years later, had carried me from Ecuador into the Caribbean. Another time I had travelled the length of Mexico on an anthropological grant. And now I was sitting in Las Vegas, New Mexico, in the furthest reach of the Hispanic territory. Over the years, unwittingly, I had been making a journey right across the Latin world. And now, finally, it was ending. The next state east from here, just a couple of hours away, was Oklahoma. The next one north was Colorado, an alpine, white-populated state. This was it: I had come to the end of the Spanish New World. The journey was over.

It was like coming to the end of a long book. I would close the cover soon, go home, and for years I would be able to feast on the memories, discover slowly, in pieces, what the Latin world had given me, what it had meant to me, why I had been obsessed with returning to it for so long, why I had so wanted to get to the end of it.

It was sad, too, to find this forlorn drunken community on the edge. There were drunken bars throughout Latin America, but here there was none of the verve of Colombian or Argentinan drinking. Placed in its context, this now seemed a dour land. It was Hebridean, compared to Venezuela's West Country, say. The drinking was patently for escape, for anaesthesia, not revelry. The music coming off the jukebox was one lugubrious ballad after another.

I was about to leave when a small man appeared beside me in the throng and introduced himself as Cliff. He was an Anglo with brown hair, long sideburns and a flowery shirt. He offered to buy me a drink, then asked where I was from. When I told him England

217

he declared that he had suspected it. Something about me had told him.

It turned out he had lived in Oxfordshire for five years, at RAF Upper Heyford. He had been an aircraft mechanic with the USAF. He reminisced a little about the F1-11s he had serviced, marvelling at their aerobatic abilities, then told me he was now an artist.

'What kind?' I asked. 'Sculptor, painter?'

'Air.'

'Air?' I wondered if he meant he was a pilot, perhaps an aerobat.

'Yeah. Airbrush. I'm an airbrush artist.'

I imagined misty depictions of dawn made even mistier by the use of an airbrush.

'I do cars mostly. Trucks too.'

'You paint cars?' So that was why he used an airbrush. He did resprays. It seemed a little far-fetched to call himself an artist, but I wasn't about to disabuse him.

'Bodywork?' I asked. I thought of that distant cousin of mine, who had himself once sported bushy sideburns, and I was about to tell the story of his having painted Tom Jones's car, when Cliff corrected me.

'No, no. Car art. Truck art. I do art on cars.'

I had seen elaborate decorations adorning a number of cars around the state – beach scenes, mountain landscapes, cartoon women in bikinis. They seemed to be popular on cruising trucks with tinted windows.

'Mostly ladies,' he said.

'Ladies' cars?'

'Ladies *on* cars.' He giggled, and for the first time I noticed that he was quite drunk. 'I mostly paint ladies for people. Sometimes trees, mountains, lakes, the ocean, whatever, but mostly it's ladies they want.'

I nodded. 'You must be good.'

'I keep busy. People like what I do. Well.' He raised his tequila shot glass.

I lifted up my beer bottle. 'Here's to ladies on cars.'

'And ladies *in* cars.' He snickered like he had just said something obscene.

We drank. Cliff disappeared in the throng as mysteriously as he had emerged from it, and I gulped down the remains of my beer.

Outside the temperature had dropped. I buttoned up the collar of my jacket and walked over a couple of stoplights towards a neon sign up ahead saying: 'Bar Las Vegas'. I thought I'd stop in for one more drink before making my way back to the Plaza Hotel.

But it wasn't so easy. The sign was switched on, and the double glass doors beneath it were unlocked, but when I pushed them open they led into an empty, unlit marble hallway, a long crescent with closed-up shops on one side and a wall of glass on the other. Half-way down were more double doors, heavily chained with two padlocks. I tried to look through their tinted glass but couldn't make anything out inside. Further up the walkway a light was on, so I made for that, and came upon a small room, temporary-looking, constructed out of chipboard, with a counter in front and a window so you could see in. Inside a young man was seated on a plastic chair watching a portable colour TV. He got up to fiddle with the aerial, then noticed me and walked over. He leaned down and spoke through a gap between two of the panes of glass: 'Qué hay?'

He was friendly-looking, with a scrawny beard and a T-shirt with an elaborate picture of a parrot on the front, and the words 'Costa Rica Linda' beneath. He smiled at me, revealing a gap between his front teeth.

'Donde esta el bar?' I asked.

'El bar?' He hesitated, as if he hadn't fully understood me. 'Qué?'

'El Bar Las Vegas,' I said.

'Ah.' He nodded, smiling again. 'Sí, sí. Cerrado. Cerrado.' He drew a finger across his neck. 'Ya no hay. No existe ya.'

The bar had closed down. But I was intrigued by this place. Why was there a row of shops here in this arcade? And this young man seemed to be a night-watchman of some kind. For what? Beyond him, in his little room, I could see a wall covered with pigeon-holes, like a hotel reception, although otherwise the place hardly looked like a hotel. I asked him what he was doing here.

Sure enough, he was the night-watchman, and the place had once been a hotel, years ago, but now only had long-term guests. A week cost sixty dollars, he told me, a month two hundred. He asked which I wanted.

I explained that I was only looking for a drink.

He laughed. Something about him didn't seem quite like a local. He was skinny and tall, and had a kind of energetic spontaneity in his movements, all of which were different from the typical measured, stocky poise of New Mexicans. I asked where he was from, guessing, what with his T-shirt, that it might be Costa Rica.

'Panama. I moved here two years ago.'

From Panama City to Las Vegas, New Mexico, seemed an odd move. I asked him about it.

'With all the troubles in Panama my family moved to Costa Rica.' He tugged at his T-shirt by way of illustration. 'Then I come to America to work with my cousin in Las Vegas. I take the bus through Honduras, Guatemala, Mexico, all the way, then Texas, then New Mexico. I didn't have money.' He pulled out a pocket of his tracksuit pants, turning it inside out to make his point. 'Only money to reach Las Vegas. When I get to El Paso I buy the bus ticket to Las Vegas. I have just a little money left, but the next day I seeing my cousin, so I think, OK, I go out tonight.' He laughed, and jabbed his thumb at his mouth, indicating a night on the town. 'I spend all the money. And the next day the bus take me here, to *this* Las Vegas, the *wrong* Las Vegas. But I had no money left.' He made the move with his thumb again, laughed apologetically. 'All gone. So I cannot buy the ticket to the right one. So I work here.'

First he had bussed in the Bar Las Vegas. The manager had given him one of the long-term boarding-house rooms upstairs, which he described as a prison cell, and very cold. He had never felt cold like it, he said. Then when the bar closed down he had landed the job as night-watchman.

'Is good here. So I stay.' He shrugged his shoulders. 'I just stay.'

'And your cousin?'

'Is OK. He know I am here. I write my family and tell them everything.'

'You like it here?'

He nodded. Then he laughed, remembering something. 'I write my friends in Panama. I tell them I am living in Las Vegas. They very jealous. They all want to come here and work too.' He flicked his hand down in a Latin gesture of accomplishment, chuckling. Then he frowned defensively. 'But is true. I *am* in Las Vegas.' He shrugged again.

I laughed at his little scam, which seemed to be the response he wanted. Then I asked, 'Are you planning on staying?'

He screwed up his face. 'Quién sabe? Quién sabe, señor? The only sure thing is we are all going to die, no?'

I agreed, enjoying his fatalism.

He advised me not to go to Murillo's bar, if I was still looking for a drink, and instead recommended the bar of the hotel where I was staying, then went back to his TV set, wishing me luck.

I went home to bed.

The next day was similar. I let the time drift by. I strolled about, I sat in the diners having three prolonged meals, I read one of my new collection of James Bond books, hitting by accident on *Diamonds Are Forever* which I had forgotten takes place in Las Vegas, Nevada. It almost made me want to go there. It certainly made me want to drink bourbon and to start smoking again, both of which I did that night. I sat on a stool at the bar of the Plaza Hotel and ordered a Wild Turkey on the rocks. It was so good, and slipped down so easily, that I quickly ordered another one, then found myself eyeing the Winston pack of the other man sitting at the bar, three stools along from me. The smoky flavour of the bourbon called vehemently for a mouthful of smoke. It wanted to be wreathed in blue clouds, as if it would only be complete once it was surrounded by a smoky envelope.

On the other hand, I hadn't smoked in a while and I knew it was a bad idea to give in. I did anyway, but instead of buying my own pack I decided I would ask the man for one. I doubted I would have the gall to ask for more than one, so it seemed a safe plan.

He obliged. Twenty minutes later, after my third cigarette and my fourth bourbon, I was at the cigarette machine thinking to myself: what the hell, I'm in Las Vegas, in New Mexico, who cares, James Bond could smoke and drink and look what he did, so why the hell can't I?

It wasn't much of a night. No one else came into the bar. I tried to engage the barmaid in conversation once or twice, or possibly more, possibly too many times, and ended up going to bed early.

In the morning my chest and head ached equally. I lay in bed reflecting on the lonely drunken Englishmen I had met here and there on my travels who had left England decades ago, in their twenties, full of promise and hope, and who had washed up over-weight, middle-aged, red-faced, on bar stools in the tropics, clad in damp Hawaiian shirts. It occurred to me that they might have read James Bond books in their youth, and been inspired by them to go off to work in exotic lands. It seemed amazing, in fact, that more people hadn't succumbed to the allure of those books, and gone off in search of the James Bond life. Or maybe they had, but had discovered it was a shallow thing, and anyway that there was more to being James Bond than airports and cocktails. You had to have joined the Navy at sixteen, for a start. Maybe people were wiser than I thought, or maybe aches in the head and chest like I now had were effective deterrents.

I hadn't drawn the curtains the night before, and I could see a clear, sharp blue sky outside, a little daunting for one in my condition. But then I remembered today was Sunday, and somehow that made it feel easier. I had a shower, then a long breakfast of huevos rancheros in the restaurant downstairs, mopping up the sauce with flour and corn tortillas, then went out to the Bronco. To my surprise, it wouldn't start. It didn't even turn over. When I turned the key all it did was click, and a red light on the dashboard came on. I tried it a few times. I wondered what to do. I went and sat in the hotel lobby pondering the situation. I had taken two aspirin, so my head hurt less, but it wasn't exactly clear. I felt not so much unnerved or frustrated as baffled. It seemed entirely perplexing, almost intriguing, that the Bronco wouldn't start. It occurred to me that it might be some kind of omen. My plan, formulated at some point in the middle of last night, had been to prowl the churches of Las Vegas this morning. It had seemed a good plan and it still seemed a good plan. It was Sunday, I could catch the Flying Father at work, which would be the most natural way of all. I stumble upon his church, I congratulate him on the sermon afterwards, and reveal that I remember him from years before. That way I wouldn't seem like some prowler who had been stealing up on him. Who knows, he might even have felt intimidated to have me present myself at his door. All I had to do was take in a good number of churches between nine and twelve and I was sure to find him.

It was already nine forty-five and now my truck wasn't working. I wondered why this had happened. Was it a bad idea for me to chase up the Flying Father, and was this a benevolent universe after all? It crossed my mind then for the first time that he might be dead. The thought sent a shiver of dread through me, but the shiver left in its wake a sense of openness and freedom, a reminder that life was not long and therefore it was good to get on with the most important things, and that in some obscure way I was beginning to do that, now that I had come to New Mexico.

I went back to the Bronco to inspect things more closely. I tried to start it again, just in case it had changed its mind, and mysteriously it at once shook into life. I sat there behind the wheel feeling it tremble as it warmed up, with a faint smile on my lips. I wondered if perhaps I had not turned the key far enough before, but knew that I had. It seemed strange and exciting, as if I had stepped into a slightly different world from the one I was accustomed to, like a parallel universe.

It didn't take me long to find the right church. It was the first one I came to: down the main drag from the plaza, past the shut-down Hotel Las Vegas, and on up a little hill to a grassy knoll on which stood a brick Catholic church. I parked and looked at the notice-board. Padre Rodriguez García, it said.

There was no one around outside. A mass was going on. I walked up the steps to the white door and carefully opened it a crack. Immediately it swung all the way out and a woman's face appeared, framed in white curled hair and ivory earrings. Her eyes sparkled as she welcomed me in.

I stepped forward and whispered to her, 'I'm looking for someone.'

She nodded at me, then smartly stepped outside, holding the door to keep it from banging.

'Whoever you're looking for, I'm sure He's looking for you too,' she said in a soft, harmonious voice.

Sensing that her *bon mot* hadn't quite come off, she went on, 'I'm Blanca Carmen.' She held out her hand. 'Tell me more. Then join us for mass. Do you take communion?'

I didn't have the heart to say I wasn't a believer, and mumbled an affirmative, immediately going on to say that I was looking for a certain priest who I believed was currently working in Las Vegas, and did she happen to know which church he ministered in. I described him.

She nodded as I spoke. She had a strong, angular face, which didn't go too well with her soft, white ringlets. Her eyes were a gleaming coal black, and she had a fine down along her top lip, picked out by the morning sun.

'I certainly do know him,' she said. Then she took hold of my forearm. She had a strong hand, thinner and tougher than I would

224

have expected, and held me firmly but warmly. There was something oddly reassuring about the grip. It made me feel young and tender and happy all at once, like a child reunited with its mother. She cocked her head a little and looked into my eyes. 'We all knew him here. This was his church. So you've come to the right place.' I noticed that her eyes were glistening now. I felt curiously close to her, and for some reason I was happy to be standing outside this particular church with that particular gang of people I had barely even glanced at sitting within, and to be beside this woman.

She sighed, still holding me. 'So you haven't heard, then.'

I looked at her and knew then that it was true, even though she hadn't actually formed the words.

'It was very sudden. He was flying up to South Dakota and ran into a freak storm over the mountains.'

I looked down, not sure how to react. The woman moved her hand along my arm and gripped my fingers. It was a cool, tender grip. Somehow her treating me with such concern, as if I were a close friend of his, neutralized whatever might have been my real feelings, and instead I felt fraudulent, as if I were some impostor masquerading as the man's heir. I said, 'I'm very sorry and sad to hear that.'

'It was such a shock to us all,' she said.

'When was it?'

'January.' She shook her head slowly. 'They have some fierce storms in January out in these parts. Some said he shouldn't even have been flying. But he knew what he was doing. He was always flying. He had the Lord's work to do. Nothing would stop him.' She paused. 'Did you know him well?'

I told her I had met him in Vermont.

She smiled. 'In the Morrisville Congregation?'

I smiled back uncomfortably and said that in fact it had been at the airport. I added with a chuckle that I had filled up his plane a few times, hoping it might come across as some kind of joke.

She nodded. Then she shook her head. 'It's been a great loss.' She closed her eyes. 'Such a fine man. But now the Lord has taken him unto His bosom.' She breathed in and out, tightening the grip on my hand, pulling it into her stomach. Then, after a suitable pause, her eyelids fluttered and she opened them up again. 'Would you care to join us for the rest of mass?'

I thanked her. I didn't really see any way I could refuse. And anyway, it was the least I could do for the memory of the Flying Father. I said, 'I'll just sit at the back.'

'Very good, then.'

The back pew was empty. I forgot to genuflect and cross myself as she did when she entered the church after me, so I made up for it by getting my head down in the prayer position for a minute as soon as I sat down, hoping she noticed. Then I realized that I was wanting her to notice, and reminded myself that a man I had once admired had died. He was gone, and would never come back. Nothing was left of him. His life, his existence, his being were over. Such was life. You blinked and it was gone.

I talked to myself in this vein for a while, hoping to feel appropriately solemn, yet somehow it didn't work. I couldn't help feeling light-hearted, even flippant. At one point in the service I even came close to laughing, and had to fight down my giggles. When the communion started I got back down into my prayer position to avoid the embarrassment of being invited to join in and either refusing or illegitimately accepting, and then discovering that I didn't know the correct procedure. It worked. No one disturbed me. My prayer was respected.

I left promptly at the end. I didn't think about what to do next. I didn't need to. I acted automatically, driving back to the hotel, checking out of my room, leaving Las Vegas for the freeway once more, and pointing the big square hood towards Santa Fe. Santa Fe was where I was going. Joel the sculptor had his life. He would be busy tunnelling to his dying day. The Flying Father had had his life, an austere, rich, strong life, as it had appeared to me, and he had met a fitting end, high in the skies over New Mexico, his plane probably cracked in two like a toy by a thunderbolt of the Lord's. And now I was driving a truck west along the highway towards Santa Fe. I wasn't sure what I would do now, but whatever it was I knew it would be the start of something big.